Praise for the First Edition of
Parenting Your Dog

"Like all great ideas, this one is blatantly obvious—
after Trish King came up with it! The Einstein of
practical and humane training, Trish King has done
us all a favor by connecting the dots between the
two- and four-legged members of our families in
ways that will make everyone happier!"
—Patricia McConnell, Ph.D., Certified Applied
Animal Behaviorist and author of
The Other End of the Leash

"Covers territory that dog owners and future
dog owners will find invaluable: that elusive
combination of training, behavior, and the
intangible but critical importance of what it really
means to live with a dog."
—Sue Sternberg, author of Successful Dog Adoption
and owner and founder of Rondout Valley
Animals for Adoption

"Perfect for pet owners...this book will certainly
help those who own dogs, are thinking about
getting a dog, and even those who are starting a
'human' family!"
—Pia Silvani, CPDT, Director of Training and Behavior
at St. Hubert's Animal Welfare Center

"Includes...practical and lifesaving exercises and
tips that will likely become 'gems' in the world of
pet dogs and their people. Her work so clearly
illustrates that the behavior you can change is your
own."
—Mary Lee Nitschke, Ph.D., Professor of Psychology at
Linfield College, Director of the OTIS (Owner Trained
Individualized Service Dogs) program,
and Animal Behavior Therapist

Parenting Your Dog

Develop Dog-Rearing Skills for a
Well-Trained Companion

Trish King, CPDT, CDBC

Parenting Your Dog

Project Team
Editor: Stephanie Fornino
Indexer: Elizabeth Walker
Designer: Stephanie Krautheim

T.F.H. Publications
President/CEO: Glen S. Axelrod
Executive Vice President: Mark E. Johnson
Publisher: Christopher T. Reggio
Production Manager: Kathy Bontz

T.F.H. Publications, Inc.
One TFH Plaza
Third and Union Avenues
Neptune City, NJ 07753

Printed and bound in China
10 11 12 13 14 15   1 3 5 7 9 8 6 4 2

The Library of Congress has cataloged the hardcover edition as follows:
Library of Congress Cataloging-in-Publication Data
King, Trish.
Parenting your dog / Trish King.
p. cm.
Includes index.
ISBN 0-7938-0548-1 (alk. paper)
1. Dogs-Training. I. Title.
SF431.K558 2004
636.7'0887--dc22
2004010417

This book has been published with the intent to provide accurate and authoritative information in regard to
the subject matter within. While every reasonable precaution has been taken in preparation of this book, the
author and publisher expressly disclaim responsibility for any errors, omissions, or adverse effects arising
from the use or application of the information contained herein. The techniques and suggestions are used at
the reader's discretion and are not to be considered a substitute for veterinary care. If you suspect a medical
problem, consult your veterinarian.

Note: In the interest of concise writing, "he" is used when referring to puppies and dogs unless
the text is specifically referring to females or males. "She" is used when referring to people.
However, the information contained herein is equally applicable to both sexes.

The Leader In Responsible Animal Care For Over 50 Years!®
www.tfh.com

Table of Contents

Foreword

"The possibility that animals have
mental experiences is often dismissed
as anthropomorphic...But this
widespread view itself contains the
questionable assumption that human
mental experiences are the only kind
that can conceivably exist. This belief
that mental experiences are a unique
attribute of a single species is not only
unparsimonious; it is conceited."

—Dr. Donald R. Griffin

THE QUESTION OF ANIMAL AWARENESS: EVOLUTIONARY CONTINUITY OF MENTAL EXPERIENCE

When I was pregnant, I sometimes felt like public property. Women I'd never met walked up to me, put their hand knowingly on my belly, and pronounced the sex of my child. They told me whether I'd have an easy (or hard) birth. To my chagrin, I learned much more about the birthing process than I ever wanted to know—emergency hysterectomies, six-day labors, months of recovery. Later, after the birth, other people seemed to feel quite free to pronounce judgment on my parenting skills, good or bad (mostly bad).

New parents become familiar with the experience of trying to avoid grocery store shoppers who glare at their screaming child (attempting to get at the candy) and then at the parents for not controlling her. It's embarrassing. Even more embarrassing is traveling on an airplane alone with your cranky kid. There's no one to "share" the experience with or to hand the child to as you take refuge in the restroom.

Then there's the touchy–feely stuff. Some people aren't content with just holding the baby's hand or feeling a cheek. Some clutch at babies, trying to wrench them out of your arms, or they take off their booties to see their cute little toes. Altogether, it can be an alarming experience!

Oddly enough, the same kinds of things happen when you have a dog (well, not the pregnant part). Sometimes it seems like everybody wants to hold your puppy or little dog. They pull him from your arms, even if you don't want them to! If your dog is too big for cuddling, strangers reach down to pet him, often scaring the heck out of him. Suddenly, everybody's an expert. People who have never owned a dog are more than willing to give you their best advice. They instruct you on how to housetrain your puppy and how to stop him from chewing, digging, or using your arm for teething purposes. They even tell you how to stop your dog from biting and what to do with him if he doesn't stop.

There are some very strong similarities between parenting a child and parenting a dog, and if you've already had a child, you possess a lot of valuable knowledge of which you may not be aware. With a little adjustment, many of your hard-earned skills can be used in raising your dog. I decided to write this book because many of my clients told me they were using their new dog-training skills on their kids—successfully. A few clients even jokingly offered to pay me to train their children. After finishing a consultation, other clients would remark that training their dog was just like raising their children—if only they'd known this before! In fact, if dogs weren't animals, we wouldn't be talking about "training" them. We'd be talking about raising them and teaching them good manners. If this is anthropomorphism, then I confess that I am an anthropomorphist. However, I'm in good company.

Introduction:

Understanding the Human–Canine Relationship

n the beginning, dogs were most likely considered pests who skulked around villages waiting for leftovers. These dogs were very much like our dogs today who hang around the dinner table or the baby's highchair. In a way, dogs domesticated us because they discovered we were useful as a source of food and comfort.

As the years passed, a symbiotic relationship developed between people and dogs. We enhanced dogs' talents as drovers, herders, hunters, and protectors in return for food and comfort. Consequently, their value increased—or at least the value of some of them. Other dogs were killed, culled, or ignored. Pariah dogs, or village dogs who belong to no one, still exist today, mostly in third-world countries. And of course, our more "civilized" society also discards dogs, mostly as a consequence of overpopulation.

From pariah to worker, dogs were increasingly viewed as "tools," helpers in the business of living. Mostly, these dogs lived outside, waiting to do their jobs in exchange for the rewards that followed: food, warmth, and a little attention. Chances are, puppies were cuddled and loved for their cuteness (all babies are adorable, as we know), but grown-up dogs had to earn their keep. This is not to say that they weren't appreciated; in fact, there are hundreds of stories of "man's best friend"—loyal, affectionate, and steadfast—that persist through the ages to the present day.

As the millennia wore on (estimated at between 17,000 and 100,000 years), we humans concentrated on breeding more of the type of dog that we wanted and less of what we didn't want. Essentially, we took some of the behaviors and attributes of the parent species (the wolf) and "adjusted" them for our own ends by selectively breeding dogs who exhibited desirable attributes and not breeding those who didn't. Some examples of this adjustment include:

❖ Wolves stalk their prey, sneaking up on a deer, for instance, to give the pack the best chance for a kill. When playing, dogs also "stalk" other dogs or people. We humans have modified that behavior in our retrievers and hunting dogs—they "point" toward their prey. Herding dogs also "stalk" sheep or cows.

❖ A hunting pack of wolves might surround a herd of deer and then isolate a specific animal they intend to make their dinner. Sheepherders use these behaviors to help round up their sheep (without thought of dinner). Many of our dogs love to circle anything, including cars, bicycles, sheep, and children.

❖ Wolves take pieces of their "lunch" back to their pups in a den. We use this behavior to encourage our dogs to fetch a ball or flying disc and (with any luck) to bring it back.

These selective practices could be called breeding for function, and they led to the wide variety of dog breeds that we know today.

Nowadays, of course, most dogs don't do anything particularly useful at all. Most breeders don't breed for function (herding, droving, hunting, etc); instead, they breed for form (beauty), a practice that has given rise to dogs who look great but who cannot effectively do their original jobs. These dogs often display health or behavior problems as well. Most of us love our dogs for who they are, not what they do. They are our companions, our children, and the objects of much affection,

Today, most dogs are valued for who they are, not for what they were originally bred to do.

largesse, confusion, and frustration. However, it's very important that you realize that breed-specific behavior can make a big difference in the puppy or dog you pick. For instance, if you don't want a dog who is driven to herd, then you should avoid getting a Border Collie, Australian Shepherd, or other herding breed. If you want a dog who will retrieve, then choosing a Labrador Retriever or Golden Retriever might be the way to go.

DOGS ARE FAMILY ANIMALS

To us humans, the most important part of dog ethology (study of dog behavior) is the dog's need to be a member of a pack. He's a family animal. Did you know that a wolf pack is pretty much an extended family? It is. Did you know that wolves cooperate in raising their young? They do. It's sort of an "it takes a village" approach to child raising. Think of a human family; when we're at our best, we use the same approach—both parents

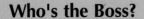

Who's the Boss?

Many books on dog training focus on the human taking over the position of "alpha" in place of the head wolf. In popular mythology, this "alpha" is a powerful figure, even god-like. He rules with his teeth and lets all the other dogs in the pack know through threatening signals what they can and cannot do. Some books or trainers instruct owners to show the dog who is boss by turning the dog over and pinning him. This is supposed to demonstrate to the dog your extraordinary power and physical strength, but in my view, it is just not necessary. In fact, if you have a large dog and you're not very strong, it's not even possible.

While it is true that every social group needs a leader, this leader doesn't need to be punishing and aggressive. In fact, a good leader might easily be nurturing, caretaking, even manipulative, and be just as successful—a tolerant parent who sets reasonable rules and makes sure that they're followed.

cooperate in raising children, as do older siblings. And in many cultures, grandparents, aunts, and uncles are involved.

When a child is raised by a family, there is and should be a great deal of trust placed within family members. Young children should feel free to explore their world, knowing the adults will be right behind them keeping them safe from harm. This relationship allows children to indulge their intelligence and to experiment with all of the senses in a caring environment, which will potentially lead to rapid learning.

The same would be true of a dog family, assuming we allowed this process to take place. Although male dogs are dissimilar to male wolves in that they don't play a role in nurturing, female dogs are quite supportive in their parental duties. They allow experimentation and exploration and stop their puppies only when they get too rowdy, too rough, or stray too far.

As children grow older, we expect more of them. They begin to take part in family chores (at least we hope that they do) while continuing to be motivated to learn. At adolescence, they begin to break away from their family and may challenge authority in a variety of ways—piercing various body parts comes to mind at the moment, along with tattoos. It's at this point that kids might join gangs or form cliques of their own peers. When adolescence ends, children are ready for the responsibilities of adulthood if they have survived. And most do. In fact, most grow up, marry, and have kids of their own.

So it goes in an intact canine pack. Adolescent dogs are challenging, to say the least. In a wolf pack, this may be the time the young wolf splits off from the main pack. Or he may stay and adjust his behavior to fit in. No matter what the world, adolescence seems to be difficult for both the individual and the family, but they both get through it.

In order for the family to function properly, cooperation is imperative. The cooperation stems from need—it's substantially easier to be a good hunter when you have an effective support system. And most communities (packs or families) have rules to help the social structure stay in place. Another necessity is that some kind of consequence,

Your dog needs a nurturing parent who also knows how to provide structure.

either for actions that break the rules or for actions that are desired, must exist. A consequence for a child who behaves inappropriately might be a time-out. The same consequence can apply to a dog who has been naughty. Of course, rewards are appropriate for good behavior. One of the most important things about a consequence is that it should not be a surprise. Both children and dogs should be clear about rules and consequences, and I'll be discussing types of consequences throughout this book.

DOG TRAINING

Traditional dog trainers, especially those who train either for hunting or for the military, tend to view dogs as tools. They decide what job they want the dog to do, breed dogs specifically for that job, and then train them to do it. For example, obedience-trained dogs are taught to walk on the left side of the handler. Why? Well, because hunters and soldiers carry their guns in their right hands! Thus, if traditional trainers desire a retriever but have a dog who doesn't want to retrieve, they may use techniques that can be quite painful to the animal. However, these kinds of methods do work in most cases. If they don't, the dog may be discarded because he is considered "flawed" in the eyes of his trainer. When you are training with a specific goal and the dog is your tool, you might not be worrying about how the dog "feels" about the training. I still remember being told that a correctional "pop" on a choke chain was necessary for training purposes and didn't hurt the dog, even if he yelped. In my ignorance, I even told other people the same thing.

In the last few years, dog training has progressed a great deal, and many wonderful trainers are instructing with their brains rather than with pain-inflicting methods. However, training is only a small part of the art of raising a dog. Your relationship with your dog is much more important. Your dog should want to be with you, want to please you, and know what is appropriate and what is not. He doesn't need a dog trainer for a leader—he needs a sensible, nurturing parent who knows how to sustain a loving relationship while providing the structure he needs. If you've had to manage a houseful of kids and have launched them into the world, you probably have the skills to teach a dog how to get along in your family and in society.

At the same time, though, my experiences have taught me that many people have unrealistic expectations of their dogs. They might remember having a dog as a child—maybe when Mom was home all day to take care of him. Or they envision dogs like Lassie or Rin Tin Tin, fully trained and ready to risk their lives for their people. Countless numbers of people complain to trainers that their dog won't come, as though the act of coming to the human is intrinsic to the animal (it isn't). We oftentimes expect perfection and ask the impossible of our dogs: to accept rude or cruel behavior from other dogs and from people, to never lose their temper, to never make a mistake. It's important to remember that parenting your dog is all about realistic expectations and a little knowledge of dog behavior. Dogs aren't children, but the two "species" have a lot in common, and good parenting skills will always be in demand.

I've split this book into three broad sections: "Puppyhood," "Adolescence," and "Adulthood and Aging." (There is also an appendix on problem behaviors.) Occasionally there is some duplication of information. However, I did write this book to be read as a whole, and I believe that dog parents might find it useful, interesting, and hopefully, entertaining.

Puppyhood:

Eight Weeks to
Five Months

Part 1

Chapter One

Choosing a Puppy

I f you're considering acquiring a puppy, I suggest you first take stock of your life to see whether you're a good candidate for one of these furry dynamos. Families and homes best suited for raising a puppy meet most of the following criteria:

❖ The parent or caretaker is home much of the time. (No workaholics allowed—pups can't handle 8, 10, or 12 hours alone, certainly not without being lonely and destructive.)

❖ The house has areas that can be barricaded or fenced off from other areas.

❖ Keeping your house clean is not your primary focus in life.

❖ You're not attached to your things in their current condition.

❖ You have a lot of patience, and you don't get angry easily.

❖ You understand that dogs do not speak or understand English, Spanish, or Swahili.

❖ You realize that puppyhood lasts longer than you want (about five months) and that adolescence lasts even longer (up to three years).

THE RIGHT PUPPY FOR YOU

Before you pick out a puppy, you need to know a few things about them. First, they're cute, cuddly, and adorable. You will most likely fall in love with the first one you see. However, that doesn't necessarily mean that you should adopt that one. Just as children are born with certain temperamental traits, so too are dogs. One human baby might be fairly placid, with an easygoing personality, pretty tolerant of loud noises, and able to fall asleep easily. One might be like quicksilver, nervous and oversensitive, with seemingly no need for rest. In the same way, some puppies are very tolerant of handling and noises, while others are sensitive, needy, and overreactive. Still others might be independent and intolerant. You can find out some of the puppy's traits by spending some time with him, but you have to hold your emotions in check—don't go by the cuteness factor!

Temperament

By and large, tolerant puppies grow up to be tolerant dogs, and sensitive pups grow up to be sensitive dogs. If you have a growing human family, you might want the former rather than the latter, no matter what the pup actually looks like. (After all, he won't look like that for long.) When you go puppy visiting, try to see more than one puppy in a litter, and try to see at least one parent but preferably

After you initially meet the puppy, ask if you can socialize him alone.

both. In fact, try to see the adults first so that you know what you're getting into. This is very important because a puppy not only inherits his looks from his parents, but he also inherits their temperaments. If the human parent of the mother dog says she's not good with people, you might want to check out another litter, just to play it safe. Because you're planning to spend the next 12 to 14 years on average with this dog, it's wise to set yourself up for success. You don't get to pick the temperament of your kids, but you do have the luxury of trying to pick out the best puppy for your family.

It's great if the puppy lives in the house with the breeder/parent. It's even better if the breeder/parent has children who have been playing with the puppies since shortly after they were born. Certainly, the puppies should have been handled extensively to help them bond with people. Whether they have been or not, you

CASE STUDY

CHOOSING A PUP

Susan and her teenage daughter have had several dogs and recently became interested in teaching their dogs to be therapy animals—to visit hospitals and nursing homes as a public service. They decided that they wanted a German Shepherd Dog because of the breed's intelligence and trainability. Susan did her research and picked a well-known breeder for her puppy. All seemed to go well, but the puppy the breeder picked for her seemed a bit nervous and shy. As the weeks went on, the puppy became more nervous—spooking at sudden noises and barking when she saw strange people. When I saw them in consult, the pup had a hard time connecting with me, preferring to sit under Susan's legs. I suggested that Susan return the dog, who was temperamentally not suited to therapy work. She did so, and the breeder agreed to give her another pup. This time, I went with Susan and we spent several hours with the puppies. We took each puppy away from his or her littermate, played with each one, and narrowed our choice to two. When we left, Susan had a confident, cuddly, male—not the preferred female and not the same deep black and tan as her previous pup. But his temperament was great, and he is well on his way to helping elderly people in their nursing homes.

should evaluate them as objectively as possible. (This is not an easy task because you probably started falling in love the second you saw them.)

There are a number of temperament evaluation tests to predict the behavior of dogs. So far, none have been proven to be an effective predictor of behavior. However, until there is a proven test, you might consider taking him through a few quick moves:

❖ **Ask to socialize the puppy alone:** After the initial meeting, ask if you can socialize the puppy alone, or without interference, in a room with which the puppy is not familiar. Let the puppy explore and get used to your presence and smell. Then draw him to you and pet him quite a bit—try to see if he enjoys it. Abruptly stop petting him and just observe his reaction. If he comes back for more, that's good. If he shakes you off and walks away, that's not so good. Do this a couple of times to see if you can get him to like it. The puppy who walks away is not necessarily a bad puppy; he may just be independent or reserved. This characteristic tends to run in certain breeds or breed types, such as northern dogs (Huskies and Malamutes), guard dogs (Great Pyrenees or Kuvasz), or sighthounds (Greyhounds, Salukis, and Afghans). However, dogs don't have to be a certain breed or breed type to be independent.

❖ **Hold and restrain:** Hold him by the collar and restrain him gently. This isn't supposed to hurt; you're just holding him in place against his will. If he doesn't have a collar on, hold him with both your hands around his middle. If he's small enough, turn him on his back in your arms (as though he were a baby). If he struggles briefly or not at all, then looks at you questioningly or relaxes, that's very good. If he tries like crazy to get away, or if he mouths or bites you in an attempt to remove your hand and arm from his body, that's not so good. Cuddle him a few times to see if he gets used to it or begins to like it.

❖ **Act angry:** Next, let him relax, and when he's investigating something other than you, clap your hands and tell him he's a bad boy—act angry. (I know this is hard!) If he turns to you and offers a submissive posture (like dropping to the ground, curling and wagging his tail low, or licking you) that's great. If he walks away without "hearing" you, that's not so great. If he growls at you, maybe you should consider leaving that puppy for another parent.

❖ **Check retrieving instincts:** Check his natural interest in retrieving a ball. Ball orientation is a major plus in all dogs because it helps maintain dependence, which is desirable in a dog. It's also a great way to exercise a dog when you don't have much time. Roll a ball away from you, making sure that the dog sees it. If he chases it and brings it back, you have a winner. If he chases it, catches it, and takes it under a chair or table, not to worry. That can be worked with. If he's not interested, he may never be, or you may have a lot of work to do to get him jazzed about retrieving. Once again, certain breed types are more suitable for this kind of play. Retrievers, of course, and herding dogs (like Border Collies, shepherds) tend to be the most fixated. Northern breeds (like spitzes) usually couldn't care less.

A good family dog will want to be with you, will act apologetic when you get angry (even if he has no idea what caused your irrational outburst), and will relax when you hold him close. There are other tests you can do, but these are the easiest, and they do help you get a handle on the puppy's temperament.

Leaders and Followers

If you are lucky enough to be able to observe an entire litter, you can usually figure out what role each puppy is playing with the other pups. In every group, there's a leader, there are middle dogs, and there's an omega (the guy at the bottom of the pack). Many people either like the leader because of his confident behavior, or they like the one sitting in the corner, just looking at them. My suggestion would be to pick one of the dogs in the middle rather than either of these. The leader puppy probably got that way by pushing the other puppies away from the food bowl, by grabbing toys and other "valuable" items, and often by bullying the other pups in play. He might be a great dog, but he's likely to be a challenging pet. The shy puppy in the corner will probably cringe when you try to pet him or pick him up. When you do hold him, he may burrow into your arms (and heart) and appear affectionate. Endearing he may be, but dogs with this type of temperament often learn to use growling or snapping to keep other dogs or people away from them. In fact, in my experience, timid dogs have a very good chance of becoming defensively aggressive. Bully-type dogs can be aggressive too. (See section "Puppy Personalities.")

The most important thing for you to do as a potential parent is to withhold judgment until you've really observed the puppy. It's so easy to get hooked on the idea that this is the dog for you just because he's available now.

Every puppy has a distinct personality all his own.

Small Dogs

I meet many people who want a small dog because of space constraints in their house or because their kids want a little dog. Often, small dogs aren't suitable for a family, just because they are small. They feel vulnerable and can learn to growl or bark to keep people from stepping on them. As an experiment, try spending a few minutes with your head on the floor looking up, and you'll see why they might do that. If a small dog is what you want, be very careful during the selection process. For instance, terriers can be adorable (I have one myself), but they often have short tempers and can be difficult to train unless you explain very carefully what's in it for them. Some toy dogs, like Chihuahuas, are small and look cuddly, but they often don't like to be cuddled.

Multiples

Sometimes it's very difficult to choose just one puppy. You might fall in love with two pups in the litter. However, resist the urge. It may be easier on you to get the housetraining over with in one fell swoop, but there are far more minuses than pluses to owning siblings. The first is that the puppies tend to bond first with each other, much as twins often do in the human world. They won't think they need you, and they'll have a horrible time being separated (which has to happen sometimes!). They're often twice as difficult to train just because of those two factors. And if you think one puppy can be destructive, just wait until you see what two can do!

PUPPY PERSONALITIES

Everything children do is practice for adulthood, which is why it's important to instill values and some habits as soon as they are ready for them. For some children, the nurturing instinct, as evidenced through play with dolls, may point to a future parental role. Other children, who are fascinated with tools or building utensils, may develop an interest in architecture later in life. Still other children, who display more

dominant personalities at a young age, may hold other positions of power as adults. The same idea holds true with dogs; they're preparing for their future role in life, whether it's to be the perpetual child, the worker, or the boss.

Here are some child/puppy correlations you might encounter, perhaps in your own puppy!

Mommy's (or Daddy's) Pet

Child: She seems to want to please you and tends to follow you around. She doesn't want you to be angry and will do virtually anything to prevent that. Even as a youngster, she may want to cook meals and often parents her own toys. She seems easy and compliant, but there's a manipulative component here—she is getting attention in her own fashion and loves it. She will also use your presence to order other children around.

Puppy: He'll follow you around, sometimes sitting underfoot. If you act in an angry fashion, he'll drop down to the floor, wiggling, maybe flipping over and urinating. He acts as though he wants to do everything you say. He seems to be submissive, but he's getting you to do what he wants by working you. And he wants attention! He may also use your presence to increase his courage and growl or snap at other dogs who come too close to you.

The Bully

Child: Likes to play rough! She often has a vast amount of energy and doesn't particularly want to play alone. If not monitored, she could hurt other children. She is not necessarily mean but is pretty insensitive and lacks empathy.

Puppy: Likes to play rough! He's often object oriented and mouthy. He'll jump up on tables and chairs and chew and destroy anything he can get his mouth on. He tends to body slam (run into) other puppies in play. He's not mean, but he needs to be monitored to prevent future problems.

The Sensitive One

Child: Her feelings are easily hurt, and she overreacts to other kids and adults. Loud noises can upset her. She likes to play quietly, often alone.

Puppy: He plays normally, but it doesn't take much to stop him from doing something you don't like. Usually just a disappointed voice will work. He might like playing with other puppies, but one bump from another puppy will make him scream as though he's been injured.

The Mediator

Child: Usually what we think of as a "sensible" kid, she understands that she can't hog all the attention (although she tries to by being "good"). She doesn't like disagreements and will try to intervene if people seem to be losing their temper.
Puppy: Often an easy puppy to be around, he likes to please and will check in often. If he's playing with other puppies and they get too rough, he may well put himself between the two and try to stop the altercation. This can be cute, or it can get him into trouble if the other dogs start to pick on him.

SPAYING AND NEUTERING

Should you alter your dog? And if so, when? The answers are usually "yes," unless you have a breeding plan (not just a vague wish to have puppies). Oftentimes, people are quite happy to have their females spayed, as twice yearly heat cycles are a major pain. The surgery doesn't usually change a female dog's personality because their hormones surge so rarely. (The only times I've seen major changes are in very dominant, confident females who appear to need estrogen to keep them balanced. These dogs can become what we call "doggy bitches." That is, after spaying, they tend to act like males—lifting their legs to urinate and doing so often, as well as engaging in more frequent posturing).

Neutering a male seems to stir more of an emotional response from us. After all, we wouldn't consider doing such a thing to our children! However, it's usually a very good idea. There are health benefits to altering males or females, primarily those having to do with infections and various cancers, and there are definite benefits to neutering a male. Aggression is just one.[1] Neutering also helps strengthen the bond between human and dog, as the dog will no longer feel the urge to go out on the town looking for an exciting partner. Certainly, you can have a great relationship with an intact dog—it's just easier with a neutered one. Finally, tens of thousands of dogs are killed every year because they're unwanted. We should all do our part to improve those horrible numbers.

[1] Eight out of ten aggressive incidents reported in this country involved male dogs. Six out of ten involved intact (unneutered) male dogs. (Source: Humane Society of the United States & American Dog Trainers Network)

CHECKLIST

- ❖ Analyze what you want in a dog—size, coat type, breed—before you begin searching in earnest.

- ❖ Make sure that your family is ready for a pint-sized tornado and has a well-researched plan.

- ❖ Be prepared to walk away from a shelter/breeder/neighbor without a puppy in your arms if the pup doesn't meet your criteria.

- ❖ Take the time to test a puppy for friendliness and tolerance to handling.

It's a good idea to check with your vet to determine when might be the best time to alter your dog. Some shelters spay and neuter as young as eight weeks, while many vets recommend waiting until your dog is over six months of age.

Chapter Two

Early Lessons

Babies are pretty darn selfish. When they're hungry, they want to eat, when they're tired, they want to sleep, and when they're wet, they want to be dry (or at least not wet). And if they don't get what they want, they cry. And cry. And cry. Infants of many species have the ability to vocalize for long periods—it's a survival mechanism. If you're abandoned, you need to let someone know where you are.

Puppies want to eat when they're hungry and sleep when they're tired. They too can cry for a long period—and bark, whine, and yodel if crying doesn't work. It's in nature's best interest to provide a signal to the mother telling her where her baby is and what is wrong.

Our job as parents is to ensure that our little ones are comfortable. We feed them when they're hungry, we make sure that they get the sleep that they need, we nurture and comfort them, and we keep them safe. Our babies learn that food will be there when it's needed and that we are to be trusted; we will keep them safe from harm. This bonding process takes a long time with kids but much less time (sometimes only minutes) with a dog.

Neither babies nor dogs misbehave out of evil or a desire to be bad. They have no morals and they don't know right from wrong. They misbehave (if it can be called that) because they are curious or want our attention. In any case, it's preferable that we learn to manage them so that they behave well, rather than punish them after they have misbehaved.

TEMPER YOUR EXPECTATIONS

You've decided on the puppy, and you've brought him home. If you're like most human parents, you learned about pregnancy when it happened and about babies when you had one—not before. The same seems to be true of human dog parents. They get ready for the pup after they've acquired him. Although it would be better to prepare in advance, you can still manage.

Take a journey into your imagination. You have a daughter who has reached the potty training age. Every time she has an accident in her diapers, you yell and say that she is "bad." You put her in the bathroom (not on the toilet, mind you), and close the door, leaving her in there for 15 minutes or so to do her business. When you let her out, she pees in her diapers, and you yell at her again. She should know by now that she shouldn't do that!

CASE STUDY

DOGS AREN'T "BAD" ON PURPOSE

Sometimes new owners think puppies are adults in miniature and that what you see right now is what you get. Puppies go through a huge metamorphosis, both physically and mentally, over a period of weeks. When doing a private session with one young couple, the husband insisted that the puppy was chewing up his socks and underwear for some nefarious reason. He couldn't remember his previous dog doing any such thing—and indeed that might have been true, although it was unlikely. At any rate, this gentleman was punishing the pup for chewing by spanking the puppy and then isolating her for a period of several hours. He figured the reason the pup kept chewing on his stuff was because the puppy was a) stubborn or b) paying him back for the punishment. The reality was, of course, that the socks and underwear were on the floor, smelled great, and felt good to chew. I managed to convince the owner to either close the door to his bedroom or put the items away and to give the pup chew toys and wait for puppyhood to pass.

Later, when I saw the man in class, he was happy to report that the chewing was no longer a problem. I imagine by the time he gets another puppy, he will have forgotten that this dog ever chewed too!

You decide that it is bedtime. You put your daughter in her bedroom and close the door. She cries for a while, and then all is silent. In the morning, you get up, only to find that she has colored all over the walls, pulled everything out of the drawers, and broken every breakable thing in the room. You become furious and yell at her. She cries and you feel better—she must have known what she did was wrong. After all, she cried.

Now you have to go to work. You give your daughter breakfast, then put her in her bedroom, tell her to be good, and leave for the day. The room looks like a hurricane hit it when you come home. She's hungry and crying and has made numerous messes while you were gone. You are really angry this time.

Does this sound totally and completely insane? Of course it does. Yet puppy parents all over the world have those very expectations of their pups, and the pups

Set you and your puppy up for success by having realistic expectations of his progress.

have just as much of a chance of getting it right as this little girl. Let's be sensible and set ourselves up for success!

THE NEED TO CHEW

Babies of all ages will put pretty much anything they can fit in their mouths, tasting and exploring it, regardless of whether they're teething or not. Humans are born without any teeth, and their motor skills are rudimentary to say the least, so the beginning stages of this exploratory period aren't particularly intrusive. Puppies, however, are a different story. New "puppy parents" don't even see them in their totally helpless period—by the time we see them, they're in full-fledged check-this-out mode. Eight- or nine-week-old puppies can wreak more havoc in ten minutes than a human baby can do in her first eight months—until she begins to crawl. And puppies are supposed to chew; they have to figure out what the world is made of and what parts of it are edible.

This problem has nothing to do with the dog. It's the parents who have to prepare for the onslaught or at least make quick changes after the puppy has already chewed the carpet in the family room. To prepare, take some of the advice that baby books liberally give out: Puppy-proof your house. This means confining your puppy (which you're already doing in an effort to keep his waste in one area). It also means providing many different kinds of items that he can investigate to his heart's content. You can also get yourself a nice big rolled-up newspaper with which to hit yourself when you find that you forgot to move the light cord and the little guy chewed it to bits.

When babies start to teethe, they want to chew on something resilient—it apparently feels good. They really like Mom's fingers, which seem to have just the right consistency, although if they are not available, many other items will do. In fact, there's a whole industry built on suckable, chewable, comfortable items for a baby's teething process. Puppies have that same need, and the pet industry is busy filling that need as well. Experiment to find out just what your puppy wants to chew. You don't have to go with store-bought items, though. Sometimes your puppy will tell you what he wants to chew on in no uncertain terms. When our old Rottweiler, Jobear, was a puppy, he thought wood was custom made for exercising his teeth. After he ate a portion of our redwood siding (it's supposed to be poisonous to dogs, but he didn't seem to mind), he came up with a novel solution—firewood—and we went along with his decision. If we had to leave him for more than a few minutes, we would grab a hunk of firewood out of the stack and put it in his pen with him. I worried about any possible health hazards, but all in all, it seemed better than the siding. Jobear also liked drywall—he took out a whole portion in our laundry room during a major lapse of judgment (ours, of course).

Puppies especially seem to enjoy chewing on something soft and familiar that moves—you or your other family members! Though it's not a particularly big deal when he's a tiny pup, it is a much bigger deal as he gets older and his teeth get bigger.

In addition to management tools like a puppy pen, a room, or a crate, a tie-down might be in order during this most trying time. A tie-down is a short (3–4 feet [1 m]) rubber-coated wire leash attached to an immovable anchor. An eyebolt in the wall is the best, but you can attach it to a very heavy piece of furniture. However, if you're trying to control what your puppy chews on, you may be giving him the gift of a massive chew toy. If you decide to use a tie-down, you should get him used to the restraint in small doses—5 to 15 minutes at a time accompanied by a chew toy or bone, like a Nylabone.

LEARNING TO BE ALONE

Moms and their babies belong together. For most of us, it's difficult to move our babies into their own beds or into their own rooms. There are several good books about helping your child get to sleep, which are really about helping your child separate from you, at least some of the time. I remember the wrenching feeling of listening to my baby cry and thinking, "She has to go through this," even though all I wanted to do was to pick her up. Puppies have that same need for their mom's presence and for the presence of their brothers and sisters. But they have to learn to be left alone, too, and it can be hard for both puppy and owner.

An observational study on the habits of wild dogs shows some interesting things parents do to prepare their pups for separation. This particular analysis observed a feral dog who changed dens weekly. She'd leave her puppies in the first home and go find another one. Then she'd move the puppies one by one to the new home. Each time she moved her puppies, she'd take a different puppy first (leaving him alone while she retrieved the second pup) and a different puppy last (so that pup was also left alone). This way, the puppies learned that they could be alone and still be safe.

Many excellent breeders will separate the puppies for a time every day when their eyes are open and they can respond to sounds. (This is the beginning of the

Teething puppies often like to chew on something that's soft and familiar—like your fingers. Give him an appropriate chew toy instead.

Puppy Teeth

You should discourage puppy teeth from making contact with human skin from the very beginning. When your puppy is quite young, you can try a couple of things. First, when he bites you, squeal (do your best imitation of another puppy) and stop playing with him. When he withdraws, you can begin playing with him again. Try to substitute appropriate objects for your delicate body parts.

After your puppy has reached three months of age or so, this may not work anymore. Depending on his personality, it may actually escalate the behavior. Now it's time to try method number two. First, freeze; then give him a hard look (that "mommy" look), tell him no, and wait for the puppy to back off. You can also redirect the biting to a chew toy. If necessary, put him in his crate or pen, on a tie-down, or in another room for a couple of minutes, but don't leave him there too long. He's not likely to remember what he's in his crate for, and he'll just miss the attention. Many parents use time-outs for their kids. It works with some and doesn't with others, depending on whether the child views the punishment as actually punishing. Keep in mind, though, that time-outs rarely work if they are too long.

Dogs retain the desire to explore their environment throughout their lives. However, the first few months are the most intense. If you can live through those, you're doing well!

socialization period.) They learn that they won't be left alone for long and that their human or canine parent will return. However, some breeders don't realize that this is necessary for a puppy's development.

Because many people think that it's cruel to separate puppies from one another and from their mother, you may discover that your puppy has had no experience with being left alone. It's up to you to teach him, and you should start right away, but carefully. To better prepare your new puppy for separation from you, his surrogate parent, try not to spend every waking minute with him. It's tempting to play with your dog until he's sleepy and then do your chores when he's napping. Instead, try putting him in a playpen (puppy pen) for a brief period every hour or so; help him learn that you will always return. He has not been abandoned after all! Starting off this way will prevent major separation problems later—and believe me, the problems can be horrendous. They can include massive destruction, whining, barking, crying, and escaping, and they are not simple to fix.

At night, if you don't intend to have your adult dog sleep on your bed with you, then you should probably refrain from having your puppy do so. This doesn't mean that you have to relegate him to the garage (a place I very rarely recommend). Instead, put his bassinet—er, crate—right beside your bed. Give him a soft blanket to lie on and some stuffed toys, and help him settle down. If he cries a lot, try giving him a chew toy or treat dispenser with some puppy food in it. During the night, he may whimper. He will have to go potty in the middle of the night, and you should take him out, not put him out. If he cries when you put him back in the crate, putting your fingers through the bars will often soothe him and make him less lonely. The first night is usually the worst, so stick with it.

HANDLING

Your puppy needs to see your hands as benign. When you change a baby's diaper or give a baby a bath, you always take great care not to hurt her. When a baby is crying, you tend to pick her up and cuddle her so that she feels better. Imagine what would happen if we did all those things roughly or carelessly. Certainly the baby wouldn't see our approaching hands as welcoming—in fact, she might try to avoid being touched or picked up.

Of course, the same is true for puppies. Even though they're rough with us sometimes, this doesn't mean that we should be rough in return. After all, we're substantially bigger than they are—it would be most unfair. We can be firm, however. Your pup should love being handled by you; he should seek touch and not struggle when you hold him close, whether it's for cuddles, for brushing, or for trimming his nails. Be quite calm and matter-of-fact when you touch him or pick him up. Don't lift him up by the front legs—you wouldn't lift a baby by her arms, would you? Put an arm around his chest, and cradle his little bottom in your other hand. Make him feel good! But do handle him, and act very confidently when you do so.

CRATE TRAINING

At some point, your baby has to learn how to stay in her crib. That's where babies go down for their naps and where they sleep. Most babies don't like their cribs at first, but they do come to accept them after a while. A crate is essentially a canine crib that you teach your dog to stay in when you can't keep an eye on him or when you want him to go to sleep. There are plastic crates, wire crates, and mesh crates. The most popular are the plastic kind, but they all have their uses.

Crate training is an accepted and valuable tool for housetraining, but a crate can turn into a prison if it's misused. Except at night, a pup shouldn't stay in a crate for more than four hours at a time. Many people crate their adult dogs during the day, but I'm not in favor of this practice. To me, it's like leaving my child in her crib for ten hours and then expecting her to be civilized when she comes out. If your dog needs to be crated for that long every day, then you should probably reexamine your lifestyle.

At any rate, the following crate training method will help you train your dog to stay in a crate and will also help stop whining or barking while he is crated. It might feel as though you are reinforcing a problem behavior, but that's not really the case. Trust me.

You'll need plenty of wonderful treats (like pieces of chicken or beef). After you have put your dog in the crate, sit right next to it. Every 30 seconds or so, whether or not he is whining, crying, or barking, drop a piece of food into the crate. After a few minutes of this (or less), your dog will stop whining and begin to look expectantly for the upcoming treat. Keep feeding treats, but now lengthen the time between feedings to one minute and then two minutes. After about five minutes, stop giving him the treats and let him out of his crate.

The next session should be later that same day. Move from 30-second intervals to 60-second intervals quickly and then up to 2 or 3 minutes. Get up and move around, but keep returning to the crate at regular intervals and give your dog a treat.

At the next session, begin by giving him the treat upon entering the crate, and continue with one every five minutes or so. Lengthen the time he's in the crate and the time between treats. The treats should always cease abruptly when your dog comes out of the crate. Chances are, by this time he will be crate trained!

As a matter of habit, I like to give my dogs a "crate gift." This is a chew toy of some kind that they can enjoy while hanging out in their crate. I remove the remains of the toy when I let them out of their crates. That way, they actually look forward to some down time. You can also crate two dogs in one crate if they like each other a lot and don't mind sharing a small space. Many dogs are happier that way.

HOUSETRAINING

My mother grew up in England and had her first child during World War II. She tells of "nannies" who specialized in toilet training children before they were a year old to save washing diapers. I asked her how they did that, and she said that they seemed to just watch the children like hawks and put them on the toilet every hour or so. Essentially, the nannies spent their every waking hour anticipating when the child was ready to go and catching her just in time!

Potty training your child and housetraining your dog are the same thing. You want the child or dog to contain his waste to someplace manageable—in the bathroom for a human, outside for a dog. Actually, this behavior comes naturally

Crate training is a valuable tool for housetraining.

The Use of Treats in Training

Throughout this book, you'll notice that I make reference to treat rewards when training a puppy or dog. I thought it might be a good idea to talk about why one would use treats to elicit good behavior.

Most people would love their dog to behave well because he loves them or because he automatically knows what's right or wrong. We know that dogs don't have a human moral code, so that desire can be summarily dismissed. But the love thing deserves a bit more discussion. Yes, dogs love their owners; but in order to work for love, the owner would have to withhold it (love) until the good behavior occurred. Most people give their dog lots of love just because they look cute and are cuddly, so the majority of dogs don't tend to work for the reward of affection, especially in the beginning of the relationship. We use food because all animals need food, so it tends to be a reliable reinforcement or reward. You can also use toys or balls as a reward, and I often recommend it in the higher levels of training, but it's a bit difficult at the primary level.

over time for both species. Predators and other animals with homes or dens (yes, we're predators) tend to keep their living quarters fairly clean, whereas many prey animals that follow their resources from place to place don't worry about where they eliminate. At any rate, human parents understand that you cannot potty train a baby before she is ready; it's just an exercise in frustration. When the child is ready, however, it won't take long at all. My daughter was almost exactly three years old when she potty trained herself. I thought she should have been ready when she was two! But at 2 years, 11 months, she actually became interested in the potty, sat on it herself, and proudly did her business on her own timetable.

Similarly, trying to housetrain a puppy before he is ready is a waste of energy. Pups can't control their bowels or bladder until they're about four months old, the approximate age when their adult teeth begin to come in. Chastising him, rubbing his nose in it, or trying other methods won't work—when he's ready, he's ready. If you keep trying long enough, he will be ready, and you'll think it was your hard work that made him successful!

What do you do, then, during the weeks when your pup is not ready? Diapers are not practical for the most part, so take your pup out frequently. Take him outside to his "potty place" after he's eaten, of course, and every hour and a half to two hours. Praise the heck out of him when he does his business, and keep him confined when you can't watch him. Manage his environment to maximize your chances of success. Enclosures can range from one room (I use my kitchen) to a puppy pen (worth its weight in gold), to a crate. Accidents should be seen as your problem, not your puppy's. With very few exceptions, all dogs can be housetrained; it's usually not very difficult—really!

If you catch your puppy in the act of eliminating in the house, make a sound like you're catching your breath, scoop him up, take—not put—him outside, wait until he does his business, praise him, and bring him back inside again. Putting a dog outside doesn't teach him what you want him to do; you will only confuse him and make him feel lonely.

If you have to go to work all day, housetraining will take a lot longer than it does if you can monitor your pup. He just won't be able to make it for more than a few hours without relieving himself. I suggest leaving him in a confined area or an exercise pen and using newspaper or puppy pads when you're away. As soon as you come home, pick up the papers and return to the routine I just described. If you are using a crate, try not to have him stay in there for more than four hours at a time.

Some people who live in apartments and have very small dogs find it convenient to teach them to eliminate in a sort of canine cat box. That's fine, but realize that once you've taught your dog to eliminate there, it will be very difficult to unlearn that behavior should you find yourself living in a house with a yard.

SETTING LIMITS

As children grow, they test limits often—the limitations of their bodies, their minds, and your patience. We often have to remind ourselves that they're supposed to do that; there's something wrong if a child demonstrates no curiosity and shows no desire to push boundaries. Good parents give children plenty of challenges while making sure that they're safe. Puppies, of course, do the same thing, but in ways that we might not be prepared for. They love to play games that they control. The most common are keep-away and tug-of-war.

Keep-Away

With keep-away, the pup generally grabs something you don't want him to have and then taunts you with it. Puppy grabs a (dirty) sock from the floor, parent tries to get it, puppy runs away with it, parent chases puppy while yelling obscenities, puppy hides behind couch, grinning wildly. This is FUN. But how do you cope with this behavior?

First, of course, there's management. Put your socks in drawers or the dirty clothes basket, and keep other entrancing items out of harm's way. However, you can't keep everything out of the pup's reach, so when the inevitable happens, here's a suggestion: Treat this as though it's the beginning of retrieving (which it is).

A puppy's favorite objects are often your valued possessions. If your puppy picks up one of his toys, we don't pay much attention. But if he picks up one of our toys—a sock, a shoe, a child's toy, or an expensive watch—he gets lots of attention. He also gets chased all over the house or yard while having a blast. He probably thinks you're having a great time, too. Unfortunately, keep-away teaches a dog all kinds of things we would rather he didn't learn—that he's stronger, faster, smarter, and more agile than we are!

Before you fall into the keep-away trap, try this little trick. It will seem counterintuitive, but try it anyway. It won't hurt, and it'll probably work. When your pup grabs something of yours, instead of yelling and grabbing it back, praise him! Tell him he's wonderful, he's grand, and he's the best puppy you ever met in your entire life. Let him flaunt the item in front of you and don't reach for it. Keep praising

Puppies often play keep-away with items we don't want them to have.

him until he brings the item to you. Then, if you wish, you can offer him a treat or another toy for being so clever, but resist the impulse to take the item from his mouth unless he lets it go easily. And don't fight him for it under any circumstances. You are actually building a lovely little habit that you'll be very happy to use later: a retrieve. When he does drop the object or open his mouth so that you can take it, throw another item for him and play with him for a few minutes. After this little scenario plays out several times, he should be finding all kinds of stuff and bringing it to you. If he brings you something you want him to play with, great! Play with him. If it's something you don't want him to have, then do a trade for one of his toys and let him play with that. For the moment, it's important to play with the object without playing tug-of-war. If your dog holds onto it, tell him to drop it and then just let it go and wait for him to offer it again. If it's quite valuable, you can hold onto his collar and wait him out. If it's potentially dangerous, you may have to press his lip against his gum until he lets it go, but try not to do that too often, as it is painful and you're not really training him to drop it. If you don't want to play right now, still praise him, but get up and give him a food reward for his housecleaning efforts.

This is a win-win situation. Instead of being frightened of you or learning how fast he is, your pup is actually being trained to bring objects back to you. In addition, he's deferring to you, and he's playing with the toys you want him to have. You'll love this later, when you don't have time to take him on a long walk but you do have time to throw the ball in the backyard.

Unfortunately, many dog parents are successful at breaking this behavior, so they override their dog's natural retrieving instinct. Then they're upset when he won't retrieve a ball or flying disc—he won't because he's afraid he's doing something you don't like.

Tug-of-War

Tug-of-war has a bad rap in dog training circles. Many people think it can lead to aggression toward the owner. There haven't been any conclusive studies done on the subject that I'm aware of, but I stand squarely in the middle on this one. I actually recommend tug for some dogs, especially shy ones. It's a great opportunity to teach your puppy that objects aren't any fun unless you're involved. So go ahead and play tug, and if he won't give the object to you, then shrug your shoulders and leave.

CHECKLIST

- ❖ Prepare for your puppy's insatiable curiosity and need to explore with his teeth by puppy proofing your house and keeping him contained when you can't watch him.

- ❖ Help your puppy learn by giving him appropriate toys.

- ❖ Start housetraining right away, but be aware that most pups can't "hold it" until they're four months or older.

- ❖ Discourage mouthing or biting on people, gently but firmly.

Or find another great tug toy and play with that. He'll soon figure out that it's you who is interesting, not the toy. Later on you'll be very happy that you taught your puppy to be toy (object) oriented. It will keep him focused on you rather than other animals or people.

Tug-of-war is also a good opportunity to teach the "give" lesson. While you and the puppy are pulling the toy, use your free hand to hold a treat next to his mouth. When he drops the toy, give him the treat. Then start to play tug again. After you've done that a few times, cue him to "give it" as he begins to take the treat. After many repetitions, he won't need the treat and he'll give you whatever you want upon your request.

Chapter Three

It's a Big World Out There: Socialization

All parents want their children to get along with other people—to be polite, interested, and interesting. To this end, we take them places in their strollers from the time they're very young, and we continue to do so throughout their childhood. Once they start to walk, many parents take their kids to playgrounds where they learn to climb play structures and dig in the sand. A parent is always watching the interaction between child and environment, ready to intervene if necessary. Dog parents need to do the same thing; it takes only a moment for something to happen to scare or hurt a puppy, and a watchful parent can prevent any problems that might arise.

WHEN TO SOCIALIZE

One of the more important decisions you will make regarding your puppy is the age at which you will begin to socialize him to the outside world. At present, there are two "camps," both with legitimate points of view. The first, held by many health professionals, is that your pup should be kept away from people and other dogs until all of his inoculations are completed, at about four months. Before then, his immune system is not in place and he is susceptible to some serious diseases. The second, and the one that I hold, is that the puppy should be judiciously socialized from the time you get him, as early as eight weeks. Because of the rapid rate that puppies mature, the window of opportunity for socialization is extremely short—from a few weeks to just three months. During that time, your puppy needs to be exposed to almost everything he will experience in his life: primarily people, other animals, and other dogs. If you wait until 4 months, when he is fully immunized, it's tantamount to keeping your child indoors and away from the world until she is about 12 years old! With care, I think your puppy can be both healthy and social.

HOW TO SOCIALIZE

Socialization is really about exposure. Your puppy doesn't necessarily have to interact with all other dogs or people he meets—he just needs to become accustomed to them. If you'd like your dog to get along with cats, then he should meet them. If you'd like him to love children, then he should meet calm, well-behaved kids.

To People

Carry your dog to shopping centers where he can see what society has to offer. Let him walk around on different surfaces, as long as they appear to be clean.[1] He should feel rugs, tile, stone, stairs, etc. He should see colors and people and things that may look unusual to him, like men with beards, people in wheelchairs, on bicycles, in strollers, and wearing hats. In addition, he needs to hear myriad sounds, from the sounds of

Dogs should learn to interact with other dogs.

construction to children playing. By exposing him to the life around you, you are teaching him to accept novel situations and experiences.

To Other Dogs

Many doggy parents start with the right idea—recognizing the need for socialization—but they don't realize the part they play in the process. Many will take their young pups to a dog park or allow them to play with older dogs but then just let the dogs work out any problems that may arise on their own. This, in my opinion, is similar to taking your child to a playground, where the children may range in age from two to six, and allowing the six-year-old to bully your two-year-old. The six-year-old really doesn't know any better, and within minutes you may well have a screaming toddler. The same thing can easily happen if you allow a 4-month-old pup to play with 15-month-old dogs. Somebody is going to get hurt, and the resulting trauma can last the dog's whole life.

[1] You may wish to refrain from taking your puppy anywhere where unknown dogs are playing. There are myriad canine diseases he could contract, so it's wise to wait until he is properly inoculated against them.

Thinking logically, we take puppies from their mothers at the tender age of eight weeks for one reason only: to bond with humans while learning to live in our society. Why would we then throw that same puppy back into the canine mix with a bunch of dogs he doesn't know and who might have some undesirable social qualities? Not a good idea. On the other hand, dogs should learn how to interact with other dogs, which I'll discuss in a bit.

HUMAN INTERACTION

When you go for a walk with your toddler, you go prepared, and you don't expect your child to greet every adult human being. In fact, we adults tend to distrust certain people—often with good reason. If your child wants to meet an adult, you always accompany her, holding her hand. I suggest you do the same with your puppy. If a stranger wants to meet your puppy, don't let him run up to her; instead, take your puppy to the stranger, and make sure that he behaves appropriately.

What defines appropriate behavior? We humans like to pet puppies and adult dogs on the top of their heads, yet if you asked your child whether she liked to be petted on top of her head, the answer would most likely be no. When a hand comes down from above, we have a tendency to cringe. We like to see what's going to touch us. It's even worse for a puppy because dogs have no natural behavior that even remotely resembles a pat on the head. This gesture can be confusing to many dogs and scary to some. For this reason, when you've decided a stranger can touch your dog, ask her to pet him gently under the chin. She should also refrain from staring into the pup's eyes and from bending down over him, if possible. Put yourself in the place of a child with an adult standing over you, staring into your eyes and patting you on the top of your head. (This is not my kid's idea of fun, although it's not as bad as having your cheek pinched by some well-intentioned but insensitive person.)

PUPPY AND ADULT DOG INTERACTION

Most puppies have a tendency to rush right into a new relationship. In the litter, they crawled all over each other, with little respect for each other's personal space. As their mother weaned them, she taught them that sometimes she just wasn't "in the mood" for a puppy. She would growl a warning, and if she had to, deliver a quick air snap. Some strong-willed puppies may have received a quick but soft bite on the muzzle. Left with his mother long enough, a pup would have learned to approach

CASE STUDY

THE IMPORTANCE OF SOCIALIZATION

Parker was a prime example of a badly socialized dog. Sherri got Parker at the age of four months from a rescue. She and her husband were on their way to a video store when they saw the rescue group's display. I saw them about two weeks later, when they were still trying to figure out if Parker's behavior was normal. He barked constantly, he was afraid of other dogs, he was afraid of new environments, and he was not affectionate with Sherri or her husband.

It turned out that Parker's upbringing was a study in chaos. He was rescued from a shelter in a rural area and then sent to a foster home, and then another, and then another. By the time Parker was four-and-a-half months old, he had lived in four foster homes. At least one of the homes had a pack of dogs that had free run of the property. He had no chance to bond with any of the families, and he learned to distrust practically everyone and everything.

Sherri's visit with me launched her new career as a dog trainer, something she had no desire to be! Eight years later, we're both still trying to help Parker, who is now fine most of the time. However, he still charges dogs and has been prescribed medication to deal with his anxiety issues. The lesson to be learned here is that careful, early socialization may have prevented a lot of Parker's problems.

an adult cautiously, with submissive, placating postures to make sure that the adult realized that he came in peace.

We humans interfere with that process. Often, we restrict the mother dog's behavior toward her puppies because we misinterpret it, or we remove the pups from their mother too soon, so they don't get the opportunity to learn. The world is filled with adults of every species who have their own opinion about how puppies should behave. Your pup has to be able to communicate with them to be a successful adult dog himself. If you know some adult dogs who are trustworthy, try to set up play dates so that they can interact with your puppy. They are likely to be much more efficient at teaching manners to your pup than you are.

The relationship you have with your dog should override the relationship he has with other puppies, although you can have a lot of fun watching him play with them. Your puppy should learn that you are the source of all good things, including opportunities to play with other puppies.

PUPPY PARTIES AND PUPPY CLASSES

You realize that your puppy needs to socialize and play with other dogs as well as people, but you must exercise caution. Develop friendships with people who have dogs—not only puppies but also those friendly adult dogs who will teach your pup how to be polite. Set up puppy parties at different houses if possible. Much of the time it may not be, so puppy socialization classes are the best substitute. However, be careful when you sign up for a class. Just as you would carefully check out a day care center for your child, there are several criteria to look for in a puppy class. Primarily, you must be comfortable with the teacher and her methods. A good teacher or school should allow you to observe its classes. If this is not allowed, don't take your puppy there. There aren't any big secrets to puppy classes, or there shouldn't be.

Because puppies change so radically so quickly, try to ascertain how old the pups in class are. Twelve weeks is a fine time to start classes, but your 12-week-old is not

CHECKLIST

❖ Begin socializing your puppy as soon as you get him. Take him for short trips to shopping centers and friends' houses.

❖ Try to expose your pup to as many different types of people as you can.

❖ Don't let people overwhelm your pup with physical affection.

❖ Dog-to-dog socialization should be done early but very carefully, using only reliable older dogs and other puppies. Trauma at this age is never forgotten.

likely to do well if all of the other pups are 16 weeks old. All of the puppies there should be wearing basic collars or harnesses—no choke chains or prong collars. Some people believe that these specialized collars are appropriate for adult dogs, but certainly they are not suitable for puppies. In addition, the teacher should like puppies. (You'd be surprised how many trainers don't.) You should be able to talk with the teacher, especially if you see some kind of problem developing. And the class should not be 100-percent playtime. Puppies need to learn that good manners are necessary, even when exciting things are going on. They should begin to learn how to sit still when you ask them and come when they're called—even out of play.

Chapter Four

House Manners

Good parents start teaching their children how to be polite from the time they're pretty young, although not too young! It would be silly to teach an 18-month-old child to use the proper fork, for instance. Dogs, too, should be taught good manners as soon as they're ready, and they're ready a lot sooner than children. Your puppy needs to know fairly quickly that he needs to share, pay attention to you when asked, take food politely, greet you the way you want, and wait for you before going through a door if that's what you want.

Each of these habits is pretty easy to teach when your puppy is young, but they become much more difficult to teach when he reaches adolescence. Essentially, with most young pups, you just need to withhold attention until the puppy figures out what's expected of him.

SHARING

Ask any parent what her toddler's favorite word is, and she will likely say that it's "mine," quickly followed by the word "no." After a few months of this, parents have a few more gray hairs as they gamely try to teach their two-year-old the concept of sharing. Sharing does not come naturally to anyone—least of all a toddler or a puppy. It's not so common in the adult world either. Just ask a grown-up to lend you her car!

When Mary tries to take a toy from Johnny, Johnny is likely to respond quite violently—hanging onto the toy, screaming, yelling, and sometimes hitting or biting. Once again, children can't really do a whole lot of damage, and because childhood lasts a long time, babies can learn about sharing over a period of several months or years. Puppies can't.

Dog trainers call the desire to hold onto valuable resources as "guarding" or "possession." It's very natural, but it's also something we try to teach dogs not to do, especially with humans but even with other dogs. They should learn while the teaching window is open (if possible, before the pup is three months old); otherwise, the task becomes much more difficult. As with kids, one of the best ways to approach this is the trade-off routine. You offer the child a better toy or a cracker or cookie to replace the one she is holding. With a pup, you can offer a treat or a different chew toy, praise him for trading, or start to play a game that will entice him. You can also lure him to another area to play. If your pup has something dangerous in his mouth, you may have to remove it for his own safety. Put your hand over his muzzle and press on the gum above his upper teeth. This will cause him to loosen his grip. Now take the item and praise him for giving it to you. (I know he didn't really give it to you, but hey, you got it!) This technique is particularly useful when the item is dangerous or extremely valuable. What you shouldn't do is play tug-of-war in order to get the object from

Teach your puppy to pay attention to you by waiting until he looks you in the eye before feeding him.

the pup. He'll see this as a game and one that he can win. This will teach him that he's stronger and smarter than you are—not what you had in mind. He could also become truly possessive–aggressive as he matures.

GETTING ATTENTION WHEN YOU ASK

Your puppy's name is very important, both to him and to you. He should turn his head and look at you when you say it. This is crucial because it's difficult to communicate with a puppy or a child who's not looking at you.

The following little exercise is a great way to either establish or reinforce that behavior. All puppies need to eat, and pairing food with attention is an easy way to teach it. Think of a baby in a high chair, unable to eat on her own. Lovingly, you place food in her mouth, sometimes making a game of it. Meanwhile, you and your baby gaze at each other between mouthfuls. You can do pretty much the same thing at your puppy's mealtimes. He'll learn that you're the provider and nurturer and

that you are very generous as well as all-powerful. Your relationship will be strengthened with each morsel, and he will definitely watch you! All you have to do to connect his name with attention is to say it and then give him a spoonful of food. As your puppy learns to pay attention to you, wait until he looks into your eyes before feeding him. You're teaching the little guy to look to you for permission to eat, and you can transfer that behavior to almost anything. For instance, if your pup likes to play or chase a favorite toy, you can say his name and wait until he looks at your eyes before you throw it. This takes patience, but so does all parenting.

SAY PLEASE!

Teach your puppy to take food politely instead of grabbing it from your hand.

Small children live in the present. When they want something, they want it now, and they'll try to get whatever it is as efficiently as possible—by grabbing or prying and whining, or maybe even by throwing a screaming fit. Puppies grab with their mouths; they'll try to pry pieces of food or other treats out of your hand. If they're denied access, they will sometimes bite even harder or pick on another family member. You can teach your puppy to take food politely by withholding it until he does. To try this technique:

1. Put a tasty morsel in your hand and show it to your puppy. Now close your hand around the morsel (make a fist) and offer it to him. He'll probably try to get it out of your hand by any means possible. Some dogs will paw at it, as well as mouth and bite it. But your hand is made of steel—it should stay closed, and you need to refrain from pulling away.

2. Eventually—usually within a minute—the puppy will become confused and frustrated, and he will pull back or even sit. At that point, open your hand and let him take the food from your palm.

3. Repeat that move until he automatically pulls back and waits for you to open your hand. If you like, you can extend this behavior a bit by waiting until he looks at you before opening your hand, although this isn't absolutely necessary.

4. Once he's moving back automatically whenever you extend your fist, tell him "Say please" immediately before he withdraws and you open your hand.

5. Once your dog has learned how to be polite with a fist, try leaving your hand open, only closing your fist if he tries to grab the food. He'll probably learn this little trick quickly.

    Now let's teach him to wait politely for his dinner. Just as you'd expect your family members to wait until everyone is served, you want your puppy to wait until you're ready before he digs in.

1. Prepare some food that you know he'll like and hold it just above his head, ready to put down. He'll probably jump at you, eager to eat.

2. Wait quietly, without saying anything at all, until he sits. He will, although perhaps not as quickly as you would like.

3. When he does sit, give your puppy a bit of his food by hand. If he gets up, withdraw your hand.

4. When he sits again, give him more food. He'll get the idea pretty quickly.

5. Once he's sitting quickly when the bowl is over his head, start to lower the bowl. Naturally, he'll get up, so raise the bowl again and wait for him to sit.

6. When he does, start lowering the bowl again. He'll probably repeat his behavior, so you need to repeat yours. You may have to give him a bit more by hand to keep him interested while this is going on. Your goal is to have him sit the entire time you're lowering the bowl and to remain sitting until you say it's time to eat.

The first time he maintains his *sit*, let him eat as soon as the bowl is on the floor, but as you progress, you can withhold the bowl until he sits for a few seconds. I don't think you should torture the poor little guy by having him sit for minutes—just long enough so that he understands what's expected of him. This doesn't take nearly as long as you think it will. One or two sessions will often suffice.

OVEREXUBERANT GREETINGS

You can use the same principle when your pup jumps on you to greet you. I equate this behavior with that of little children clutching at you until you pick them up. Usually they add a lot of vocal urging along with it: "Mommy, Mommy, Mommy" might sound familiar. If it works, they'll keep doing it, long after they're too heavy for you to pick up easily. At some point, they have to learn that you're not always going to pick them up—you literally can't! With a puppy, don't pay attention to him until he stops asking for it. (This is the first stage of Zen learning—in order to get the reward, your puppy must give up the reward.) Thus, when he's jumping all over you trying to reach your face, just wait. When he stops jumping, squat to his level and give him the attention he so desperately wants. Later on during adolescence, you won't squat, but with a puppy, you need to give him reinforcement very quickly. His little brain can't hold a thought for too long. Besides, you probably want to give him attention.

Jumping up is a common problem behavior in puppies.

Here's a little trick that works with all kinds of behavior problems but especially jumping up and barking. I call it the "Stupid Mom Routine." I've used it for years with my dogs, but Leslie Nelson, a wonderful trainer, added a couple of steps that I like a lot.

1. First, put a leash on your puppy and let it drag on the floor.
2. When your pup jumps up on you, rather than reacting with anger or doing the no response bit, ask him cheerfully, "Do you want to go outside?"
3. Pick up his leash and take him to the door.
4. Put him outside, but hold the leash inside when you close the door. Count to five, then let him in and act normally.
5. He will jump up again, at which point you should repeat your question and response—always very cheerfully.

Generally, it takes just a few repetitions for a pup to get the idea that you're misunderstanding his communication, and he'll stop. Because he's a puppy, you'll have to repeat the series quite often with a variety of people before he stops jumping up.

The human element can be a major impediment to your puppy's learning, especially with regard to jumping up. Many people like the attention from the pup, and they'll tell you they don't mind the jumping up. If your pup is going to grow up and stay small, then maybe you don't care. If, however, he's going to be a bruiser, harden your heart and tell your friends and family that you're teaching him manners, and you have to be consistent. Each time he jumps up and gets cuddled and loved, he's learning that this behavior works, and it'll be that much harder to teach him to stop.

PEOPLE FIRST

I sometimes think that dogs want only two things in life: to eat what we eat and to go through doorways first. Leaving the food aside, kids often want to race through doorways first too. Think of a group of little children all trying to be the first through the

CASE STUDY

GOING THROUGH DOORWAYS

When clients come to my office, I generally ask them to leave their dogs in the car for a couple of minutes while they fetch me. This allows me to see a lot of behavior I wouldn't ordinarily see (like car behavior, greeting behavior, and leash behavior). I then escort them into my office. Thus, when Margie brought in her young puppy for a well-puppy consult, I was with her as she walked into our building. As they got to the door, they seemed to have a race to see who could get there first. Once there, Margie held the leash very tightly and more or less pushed her puppy back out of the doorway. In the process, Margie fell over herself! Luckily, she wasn't injured, and neither was her pup.

Margie and many others have been told or learned that they must go through doorways first. I think many people have misunderstood what the whole doorway thing means. It just means that the leader controls the territory. In actuality, the leader is not always the one in the front—the leader is the one who decides where you're going!

door or the first in the car (so that they can get the prized window seat). They have to learn to be polite and to sometimes let others go before themselves. The same is true with puppies. By now, you've probably guessed that the best way to teach a puppy not to barge through doorways is by waiting for the right behavior. You may have to add a bit more persuasion here, though.

1. Attach a leash to your pup, but let it drag on the floor. Don't hold it.
2. Go to the door with your puppy and begin to open it.
3. As he pokes his little nose through, tell him "Uh uh" and close the door.
4. Repeat. After a bit, he'll figure the door is unpredictable, and he'll pause before trying to go through. If you'd like him to be really polite, wait until he sits before you open the door.

Some puppies will actually try to barrel you over on their way to the door, especially as they get a bit older. For them, you can add a little drama to clinch the behavior.

- ❖ Good manners should be instilled from the time your puppy is very young.
- ❖ Most behaviors can be developed by controlling your puppy's movements and reinforcing the behavior you want.

1. As you close the door, give a gasp and move back a few feet (m). The puppy should follow you.
2. Approach the door again and repeat the procedure. Usually, by the third or fourth time, the pup is more than happy to let you go first. In his mind, it seems like there must be something dangerous out there that you—as the parent—need to take care of.
3. Now open the door and turn around, facing your puppy.
4. Back up across the threshold, squat, and call him, clapping your hands and acting happy. If he doesn't come, turn sideways in invitation. Walk with him as you walk away. Dogs feel safest going with a group, and puppies tend to follow a parent. You're being the leader just by telling him with your body where you want him to be.

   By the way, I really don't think people should always go through doorways first—what a pain that would be! My goal is to have your puppy wait when you tell him to; there's no reason why you can't tell him to wait, then let him go through the doorway before you.

Chapter Five

Exploring the Outdoors

Your puppy is learning from the time you get him home, which is why the rules you set up now will be very important later on, when he grows into an adolescent and then an adult. Remember that just because you're not teaching doesn't mean he's not learning. Besides the rules and guidelines you've set up in your household, you can actively teach some behaviors that will make life easier for all of you.

In this section, the ostensible goal is to take your puppy for a walk. But of course, all of the exercises in this chapter are useful pretty much everywhere. Full descriptions of training exercises are supplied in Chapter 11: Obedience Training.

LEASH TRAINING

We've probably all seen a child attached to her parent with a leash, but it's certainly not the norm. In fact, I'd guess that most people think it's quite peculiar. We use other contraptions to contain our kids, like strollers, buggies, or grocery-store baskets, or we walk beside them and behind them, picking up the pieces the kids leave behind. Moms expect their kids to explore, grasp colorful items (usually full of sugar and at exactly the right height for grimy little hands), put them in their mouths, and as they get older, to talk loudly about all the things you wish they wouldn't say in a public place.

Puppies need to explore too, and most people do use a leash, although leashes are as natural to puppies as they are to kids. This is to say, they are not natural at all. When you put a leash on a pup and hold it, he will often buck and fight, yelping and howling at you. Some puppies just dig their heels in and refuse to move. As far as your pup is concerned, that leash is preventing him from exploring his world the way he was meant to.

Unfortunately, leashes are necessary, and we do have to get puppies used to them. In fact, puppyhood is the best time to learn leash manners because he can learn fairly rapidly.

I suggest that you start leash training at home.

1. Attach the leash to your puppy's collar and just stand in place. Either hold the end of the leash or attach it to your waist so that you don't feel the need to tug on it. He'll soon start to pull on the leash. Just stand there and wait.
2. Eventually, he'll discover that the leash is restraining him, and he'll stop struggling and look at you. At that point, tell him he's a good puppy and give him a little

goodie. (Remember that good food makes for a good relationship!)

3. If he pulls again, repeat the process.
4. Once he's given up on pulling, take a step or two and then stop.
5. Chances are he'll pull again, in which case you should stop again.

This is a very practical lesson for him and requires him to think about what is happening. When he pulls, he doesn't go anywhere. When he doesn't pull, he does go somewhere.

An alternative way to teach your pup not to pull is to tie the leash to a piece of furniture, like a table leg. Do this a few

Puppyhood is the best time to teach your dog leash manners.

times every day, and he'll learn that pulling on the leg doesn't get him anywhere. When he stops trying as soon as you attach him, transfer your leash to several other immovable objects. You're actually demonstrating two things to your puppy: one, that pulling doesn't work, and two, that he may as well relax while he's on a tie-down. Once you've been successful with leash walking in your house, you can go outside, but don't plan on going anywhere fast unless you pick him up.

I can't emphasize enough how important it is to teach your dog not to pull when he is a puppy. It's much harder to teach leash manners to an adolescent or adult dog.

Going for a Walk

Now that you've introduced your puppy to the leash, it's time to go for a walk. You can either ask him to wait at the door, or you can hold him in your arms so that he doesn't charge through. After you've gone out the door, place him on the ground and give him time to explore.

Puppy Supplies

When you took a walk with your toddler, did you ever forget to bring along the cookies, apple juice, extra diapers, and pacifier? If so, did you panic and then go home and get the diaper bag? Chances are you did, or you were sorry you didn't. In much the same way, you'll need to be prepared when going for a stroll with your puppy. Your puppy supplies are actually much easier to carry than a diaper bag. With a pup, you need only take lots of his favorite treats (soft ones so that they can be split), perhaps a choice toy or two, and some plastic baggies to clean up his waste.

And explore he will! Puppies use all of their senses to check out the world, especially their sense of smell. Dogs tend to put their noses right on top of or into an interesting item, even if we think it's disgusting. Little kids do the same thing with their mouths, much to our dismay. Mud, for instance, holds a real attraction for young humans. Old smelly stuff has the same allure for pups. Both species have to be taught to avoid certain substances that we don't think are healthy or safe. Rather than yelling at the toddler, though, a parent will remove the child from the "attraction" (or the "attraction" from the child) and substitute something else, either a thing or an activity. Be advised that your puppy will probably strain at his leash to get to the offensive stuff. It's easiest just to back up and offer him another attraction, like a treat, to distract him. We'll work on a cue to teach him not to touch it later. Realistically, you'll never get your pup to stop smelling the roses, the poop, and anything else he can. As you walk down a road, imagine a rainbow of colors emanating from the street; each of those colors is a different smell, and the dog's nose is a laboratory for evaluating them.

Your first exploration should be done at the pup's pace, not yours. When you and your toddler take a walk, you usually have to stop every couple of feet as she checks out this new world. If you want to actually go somewhere, you should probably plunk her in a stroller. Not many pups get put in strollers, although it might not be a bad idea if you have time constraints. Otherwise, just be content to meander.

Sometimes puppies don't want to go for a walk. They're nervous and hang back, tugging at the leash or digging their paws in. Although it might work if you just made them walk, it's much more pleasant for the puppy to be given time to experience the environment, which can be pretty scary. One way to help him get used to it is to carry him 100 feet (30.5 m) or so from home and let him walk back with you. That can make him feel much more comfortable than heading out into the unknown alone.

If your puppy spooks at something, which is likely with some dogs, it's also best not to force him to investigate it. Again, let him go at his own pace, even if he seems to slide along the ground or walks in a wide arc around the offending "thing." Dogs have been known to spook at almost anything unfamiliar. You might remember your child having similar irrational fears. My daughter was afraid that she'd go down the drain while in the bathtub, so it was frustrating getting her to take a bath. And of course there's always the infamous monster in the closet! At any rate, if you don't make a big deal out of irrational fears, they will most likely go away and your puppy will be just fine.

Leashless Walking

The best time to teach your dog to walk with you without a leash is between ten weeks and four months, when he wants to follow you— before adolescence and its accompanying independence. To accomplish this, begin in your house by playing hide-and-seek. There are a few ways to play this game; you can wait until your pup is investigating something, then hide behind a door and call him. Have a party when he finds you—squeal and jump around using your

Puppies use all of their senses to explore the world, especially their sense of smell.

CASE STUDY

FEAR OF STRANGERS

Crystal was a five-month-old Dalmatian/Border Collie mix. Fran had adopted her from a family who hadn't socialized her at all—she'd been kept in the backyard alone all day. From the time Fran got her, Crystal was very wary of strangers. In fact, by the time I saw them, Crystal had lightly bitten a couple of children who had tried to pet her. To combat Crystal's fear of strangers, Fran had been advised to have all the guests coming into her home feed the pup some treats. That way, she would learn to trust strangers. Unfortunately, what it taught Crystal was that people were the source of tasty treats, but it didn't do a thing for her fear. When the person giving the treat then tried to pet her, she'd react aggressively. She did the same thing to me in my office, whether I was squatting, sitting down, or standing up. Crystal was terrified of people. I advised Fran that if she wanted to help Crystal, she should give the dog a treat when she saw a person. That way, Crystal could identify the person with good things (treats) and keep her fear at bay by not making her interact with the stranger. Within a few weeks, Crystal was looking at Fran whenever she saw a new and scary person. This not only decreased her fear, but it also elevated Fran's status to that of protector.

baby-talking voice. Or if he likes balls or squeaky toys, throw one of them in one direction, then quickly hide while he's fetching. This game not only encourages your puppy to keep an eye on you, but it also improves his retrieving skills. Like children, puppies think the game is wonderful, and they'll play it well into adolescence and adulthood.

Once he's pretty good at hide-and-seek, you can take it outside, but be prepared to teach it all over again, as this environment is pretty darn interesting—much more interesting than you. It's preferable to go to an unfamiliar locale, and of course it must be safe. You can put a leash on your puppy, but let it drag on the ground. Go for a mini-walk, and as soon as your pup begins to investigate something else, quickly run or trot away from him and hide in a conspicuous spot. This is just like Easter egg hunts for toddlers: The eggs are "hidden" in plain view to help the kids find them. When your puppy turns and discovers you, act very excited and tell him how clever he is—he just found an "egg!" Play this game a lot—you're going to love the long-term results. Rather than you following your dog as he wanders away, he will follow you. Not only have I used this technique with all the puppies I've had, I also used it with my daughter, who thought it was a good game as well. When other moms were chasing their kids down grocery-store aisles, my daughter was following me.

Encountering Strangers

To be safe in this new world, your little guy should be taught to ignore other dogs and people until you give the okay. We may want our pups to be friendly with everyone, but not everyone is friendly to puppies—or more to the point—to dogs, which puppies become very soon indeed. There's no problem with sociability, but it's best to put it in its proper perspective. Would you want your two-year-old running off to meet strange children or adults? Of course not! They have to be taught to be polite. There is a time and a place for everything. Right now, we're going to keep your puppy's attention on you. Also, as I mentioned, many puppies are cautious about new things, just as some children are. This isn't a character flaw; it is just a fact of life.

One of the best ways for these dogs to learn about the world is by viewing it through you and checking in with you to make sure that you're there to protect them. While you're on a walk, then, try not to let your puppy run up

Your puppy should feel safe when encountering strangers.

When out and about on leash, your puppy should be taught to ignore other dogs and people until you give the okay.

to strangers. Just hold him back by his collar or leash, and give him a little treat while you're doing so to reduce his frustration (especially if he really wants to get to the person). Then, after the stranger has asked whether she can pet your pup, you can allow it. Ask her to pet your pup gently. If your puppy seems frightened and cringes when approached, you can ask the stranger to stroke him under his chin or not to pet him at all.

I don't recommend having strangers give your puppy treats—all food should come from you. There are a few reasons for this. The first is that it works against what we've just been discussing: having your pup wait until you give him permission before he can greet a stranger. The second is that you want your pup to believe that you are the Controller of the Universe, meaning all good things come from you. The third reason has to do with shy or cautious puppies. Sometimes they really want the treat and will stretch out their heads and necks to get it while leaving their butts and back legs as far away as they can. They'll then grasp the treat and quickly retreat to eat it. These dogs are in conflict with themselves, and as they grow, they are the most likely to turn that conflict into aggression.

ESTABLISHING A SOLID FOUNDATION

If you spend the time and effort it takes to give your puppy a solid foundation, the work you have to do later—when your pup is five months plus—will be minimized. You'll be on your way to a well-mannered dog, one who understands that the world

❖ Help your puppy learn the limitations of his leash by attaching it to an immovable object so that when he pulls he doesn't get anywhere.

❖ Allow exploration as much as you can when going for a "stroll."

❖ Don't panic if your puppy spooks—just allow time for him to investigate scary things if he wants to.

❖ If you have a timid pup, teach him that the sight of or passing by scary objects is good by giving him a little treat as he passes them. Avoid having too many strangers give your puppy treats.

is a varied place and that he is safe in it because you're taking care of him. If you wait, thinking that "training" can come later, it'll be that much harder. Remember, like a child, your dog is always learning, whether you're teaching or not!

Even a puppy with a solid foundation can find ways to drive you crazy as he hits adolescence. An adolescent human is a contradiction in terms—sometimes confident, sometimes extremely insecure. Her ideas have not formed, but you'll never convince her of that. The same is true with your dog. If you make it through adolescence, you're (almost) home free!

Adolescence:

Five Months to
Two Years

Part 2

Chapter Six

Choosing an Adolescent

Somewhere between the ages of five and six months, your puppy's behavior will change—and not necessarily for the better. Instead of watching him like a hawk and swooping down to take him outside every couple of hours to go potty, you find that you have to pull his teeth off your clothing and your body. You discover him in the closet chewing on your very best shoes (probably one shoe from each pair), digging in the garden, or jumping up on everyone and knocking down children. He's also learned that he's faster than you are, more agile than you are, and thinks he's smarter than you are! He is not smarter, of course, and it's very important to bear in mind always that even an adolescent dog is the mental equivalent of a two- to two-and-a-half-year-old child.

During adolescence, human kids are socializing with their friends, pulling away from their families, and driving their parents crazy—being needy one minute and independent the next. Of course, we're talking about adolescence beginning at 12 or 13 years for a child and 5 months for a dog. In both cases, this stage can seem to last forever—up to the age of 18 or 19 for a child and up to 3 years of age in some dogs.

For some dog parents, surviving adolescence is relatively easy. But for most, it's a challenge. Instead of a caring, nurturing relationship, suddenly there's an adversarial relationship, and it's hard for many people to remember that the dog is not purposely defying his owner. Unfortunately, the typical time for dogs to appear at shelters is during adolescence because their owners are too frustrated and exhausted to keep them. Many people think that once housetraining is finished, the worst is over. If only that were true!

To make matters worse, young adolescent dogs are in a very sensitive learning period in which small events assume great importance. During this time, they're especially vulnerable to quick changes in the environment or to an unfortunate incident with another dog or a person. For example, your five-and-a-half-month-old puppy might suddenly spook when a leaf falls off a tree or a big rock appears on a trail. From the way your dog reacts, you'd think it was a bogeyman! If your previously confident pup seems to go haywire at times, just try to weather it through. Chances are he'll grow out of it just as quickly as he grew into it. And definitely act as if his behavior is no big deal. Laugh at the leaf or the rock, but don't make him approach it. Just direct his attention to something else. However, if your dog has been overreactive since he was a puppy, ignoring the problem may not help it go away. You could need a systematic desensitization and counterconditioning regimen. (See Appendix.)

Trauma can be a different thing altogether. A young dog who has been blindsided or attacked by another dog or threatened or struck by a human might be a changed dog forever—or take months or even years to return to normal. The same is true of a young child. One of my clients has a 12-year-old boy who was chased by an overly friendly Golden Retriever when he was about 4. The dog jumped up and licked the child's face, knocking him over in the process. The boy is still frightened of dogs. This is why it's so important for us to protect the kids, both human and canine. As they get older and wiser, trauma is

The adolescent period can be a challenge for some dog parents.

more easily shaken off. I'll talk a little later about how you might help a previously traumatized dog to recover.

THE PROS AND CONS OF ADOLESCENT ADOPTION

If you're considering adopting an adolescent dog, you might want to check out the pros and cons first, before you get him home.

The Good

❖ There's a very good chance the dog is already housetrained. Even dogs who are not housetrained can be fairly easy to teach, unless their previous owners actually impeded learning through their actions. Small dogs are usually harder to housetrain, whether you acquire them at eight weeks or five months.

❖ Oftentimes, previous owners have already trained—or attempted to train—an adolescent. It's very likely he'll know the *sit* cue, for instance, and perhaps *lie down*. If you're very lucky, he may have been taught not to beg or pull on the leash when walking.

❖ He'll have gone through at least one of his chewing stages, albeit the one that's easier to handle.

The Bad

❖ That first all-important socialization period has passed, and you normally have no idea how his previous owners handled it.

❖ He's had ample time to develop a lot of bad habits, like begging or running away when called.

❖ You'll be catapulted into the most challenging time of a dog's life without really getting to know him first.

THE RIGHT ADOLESCENT FOR YOU

If you are adopting an adolescent, there are some guidelines I suggest that you follow. Just as you can test a puppy to see whether he'll fit into your household, you can test an adolescent. Indeed, the test is very similar. Keep in mind that no test has been proven 100 percent correct in predicting a dog's personality—after all, we are talking about a sentient being and the art of behavior. Your major criteria should always be whether you "click" with the dog and whether you can envision him in your household.

Call the Dog to You

First, try to take the dog somewhere you and your family can be alone with him. Let him sniff around a bit and then call him. If he doesn't have a name or he's just received one from a shelter or rescue group, you can try just calling him "puppy." It's amazing how many dogs answer to that. Your perfect dog is one who will look up at you and trot over to you, wagging his tail and expecting a good time, not one who jumps on you and pushes you down. A dog who wants to stay with you is even better, especially if he sits in front of you and doesn't jump all over you.

Pet the Dog

After you've called him, start petting him and see how he reacts. Some dogs are eager to be petted, and some dogs are a bit more standoffish. If you have kids in your family, you probably want the dog who likes being touched, petted, handled, tugged, and pulled on. You want the ultimate tolerant dog. If he stares at you as though you're making a social gaffe, moves away, or worse, growls at you, then perhaps you should leave him for another family. A growl is the dog's way of communicating that he doesn't like what you're doing. You should also let the shelter/rescue group or owner know that he growled.

Play With the Dog

Now play with the dog. Get a little rough, maybe even pull out a tug toy and see what happens. See how excited he becomes and whether he starts behaving a bit overenthusiastically when he is excited. Some dogs actually seem to throw themselves at you, kind of like a football player. This can be hard to live with, especially if you have human children—and it can hurt! If the dog plays with other dogs like that, it also doesn't bode particularly well because some dogs take offense to being rushed or body slammed. At any rate, after he's excited, suddenly stop

While you're testing your potential adolescent, toss a toy or ball and see if he retrieves it—this is a great way for adolescents to burn excess energy.

playing and just stand there. You want to find out how quickly he calms down. The faster he calms down, the more likely it is that the dog will be able to relax in your home.

While you're testing, you might want to find out if the dog likes to retrieve, which is always a plus. Toss a toy or ball away from you, and see if he goes for it. It's a no-brainer if he brings it back, but don't give up if he just goes and gets it and takes it somewhere else. You have the beginnings of a retrieve in that behavior. An adolescent dog has tons of energy; it's wonderful if you can burn some of it off by playing retrieve with him.

You should also try to find out whether the dog is possessive—whether he guards his toys or food. If you have something that he might like a lot, like a chew toy, give it to him (with permission, of course) and let him work on it for a few minutes. Then approach him slowly and watch his behavior. Here are some signs that the dog has possession issues:

❖ He takes the chewy to the corner farthest from you or under a chair.
❖ He stiffens or growls at you when you walk close to him.

Dogs who like to share usually chew on their toy right on top of your feet or offer it to you with tail and body wagging. If you have kids, don't mess with a possessive dog! No matter how much care you take, food or toys drop out of children's hands, and you don't want the child and the dog fighting over them.

Gauge Your Reaction to the Dog

The last test is the one you have to take. Do you like the dog you see? There is no such thing as a dog who doesn't disrupt your life to some extent—usually a lot. If you don't feel a bond with the dog, you may end up hating him, leaving him in the backyard, or taking him to a shelter.

Be aware that many dogs adopted in adolescence can bond very quickly to you, sometimes within minutes. Often, they stick like glue to the first person who takes them out of a run or who pays attention to them. This can make you feel very guilty if you don't feel that the dog is right for you. But guilt is not a good predictor of a relationship. You need to make the decision after you have acquired as much information as possible. Besides, if that dog can bond to you so quickly, he can also bond to someone else.

Keep in mind that the dog's appearance can play a big part in the way he will act, if only because it shows at least some of his family tree. Different breeds were bred for different jobs, and their physical makeup can give you clues as to what a dog's ancestors did for a living. Just because he's fluffy and cute doesn't mean that he's the best dog for you. But by all means, check out the dog who attracts you the most, and then withhold judgment for a bit. Also, do explore different breed behavior.

WHAT TO EXPECT FROM AN ADOPTEE

If you've raised your adolescent from a puppy, you pretty much know his personality. But if you've just adopted him, he's an unknown quantity and you should be prepared. Some homeless dogs have two sets of problems: those stemming from their previous households and some developed in shelters or foster homes. Most of the problems are due to the lack of a consistent family life and no real rules, and most can be overcome with time and training. Destruction and general unruliness usually have to do with a dog's previous home. Often, separation anxiety and barrier aggression stem from living in a shelter. (Separation anxiety is the inability to be left alone; barrier aggression occurs when a dog barks at other dogs walking past his kennel. This can translate into dogs barking and lunging at other dogs or people walking past a home or yard.) No matter where these problems originated, it'll be up to you to try to help them disappear.

Before you adopted your dog, his eyes may have promised to love and obey you forever. Once you've taken him to your new home, however, things change a bit.

CASE STUDY

WHY DOGS NEED STRUCTURE

Many adopters feel sorry for their new dog, feeling that the poor thing had to suffer enough. These people indulge their dog's every needs, often changing their own life to accommodate their pet's. Such was the case with Emma, who had adopted a little Maltese mix from a local rescue group. When she met Trixie, the dog seemed perfect and indeed continued to be a good little girl for several weeks. She was housetrained, didn't bark when friends visited, and walked past other dogs without trying to get to them or barking. Trixie had a bowl of food at her disposal all the time. She also slept on Emma's bed—indeed, on her pillow—and whenever she wanted attention, all she had to do was jump on Emma's lap and Emma would oblige. Emma cancelled all of her dates so that Trixie didn't have to be left alone. Thus, when Emma did go out—just for a little while—Trixie didn't know what to do with herself. She barked constantly for a couple of hours (according to the neighbors), and when Emma got home, she was greeted by ripped-up pillows. Trixie had also eliminated on the carpet and on the bed. Emma was distraught, of course, and considered returning her. Instead, she saw a trainer, who brought some order into Trixie's life—predominantly reducing the amount of attention she got and making sure that the pair was separated for a time every day. Eventually, the problems were solved, but they needn't have happened if Emma had provided just a bit of structure in the first place.

The personalities of some animals stay the same. But over a period of three to four weeks, most dogs expand in their new homes—their personalities get bigger, so to speak. This is exacerbated by the fact that many parents indulge their new dogs at first, letting them get away with behaviors that will turn into major crimes later. A rescue or shelter dog often hasn't had the benefit of consistent rules and might tend to test limits or set his own rules. Problems, from destruction to barking to aggression, can emerge. Like teenage kids, newly adopted dogs need to have a good idea of their parents' expectations. From our parental point of view, the best thing to do is to set limits pretty firmly—they can always be relaxed later when you and your dog know each other better. For instance, you might want your new

CHECKLIST

❖ Adolescence can begin as early as five months and go on until two-and-a-half or three years.

❖ Adolescent dogs often lose much of their training, at least temporarily. Don't panic—just reinforce the training your dog has had.

❖ Adolescents need as much or more structure than a puppy, including exercise. (There's a saying in the dog world: The only good adolescent is a tired adolescent.)

❖ Don't feel sorry for a dog you got from a shelter or rescue group. Instead, give him the rules he needs to function in your family.

dog to sleep in a crate beside your bed, to stay in a controlled location when you go out, or to sit before eating. None of these is an onerous task, and they can all be discontinued as your relationship becomes more solid and the threat of massive household destruction melts away.

Chapter Seven

Caring for Your Adolescent

Adolescence is likely to be the most challenging time in your dog's life, just as it often is in the life of a human. Although your adolescent may look like an adult, his brain is not completely formed, and he is more likely to make bad choices than good. This is the time in a dog's life when he forgets what you taught him as a puppy—everything from *sit* to polite walking to coming when called. Especially coming when called. Adolescence is the most common time for dogs to be surrendered to shelters—their owners foreseeing a future of pulling things out of their dog's mouths, cleaning up the mess in the house, and chasing them all over creation. It's important to keep reminding yourself that this phase will pass, and you will be left with the adult dog you want—as long as you can maneuver through the challenges of teenagerhood. By the way, I used to think that I could make a good living boarding dogs between the ages of five months and two years. I still think I could, but I'd probably go crazy in the process.

DOG PRIORITIES

I may think my daughter should clean her room, at least occasionally, but she doesn't think the room needs cleaning, and besides, she has to talk on the phone with her friends or go to the mall, both of which are obviously much more important. That doesn't mean that she doesn't have to clean her room, it just means that she's not going to do it on her own. Dogs' priorities tend to be things like sniffing the next bush, meeting that other dog, rolling in poop, or playing ball. Unfortunately, they are not things like getting off the furniture, ignoring food on the table, chasing the cat, coming when called, or walking beside you without pulling the leash. From the dog's point of view, the furniture is comfortable, the bush is filled with information, the cat is there to be chased, the food needs to be eaten, and for heaven's sake, why walk beside you when everything interesting is somewhere else? Dogs have to learn what we consider good manners, even though to them they make no sense whatsoever. The fact that they can learn attests to their malleability and good humor. It's sort of like going to a foreign country and learning all of its baffling customs without being able to speak a word of the language.

To illustrate the difference between what dogs want and what you want, I've listed behaviors that I call "intrinsic"—that is, natural to the dog. Notice that humans consider many of them to be undesirable.

❖ chasing—part of hunting prey

- chewing—it feels good
- digging—great for finding goodies
- eating gross things—they taste good
- jumping on counters—there's food up there
- jumping on people—it's a greeting ritual
- keep-away—controlling the family pack
- picking up dead things—they smell good
- playing roughly—learning who is the strongest member of the family
- rolling in gross things—they feel and smell good
- sniffing everything—investigating what it is and who was there
- tug-of-war—taking down prey

Now, in contrast, here's a list of nonintrinsic canine behaviors that are considered highly desirable by humans:

- coming when called
- dropping that dead thing

Dogs often have different priorities than their humans want them to have.

- ❖ lying down and staying there
- ❖ no jumping
- ❖ not touching that stuff
- ❖ sitting down and staying there
- ❖ waiting at doorways
- ❖ walking nicely on a leash

Do these behaviors seem familiar? They should because they are the basic exercises of virtually every dog training class in the United States.

LIMITS AND STRUCTURE

Teens and dogs not only need structure to help them grow up to be acceptable adults; they actually *want* structure because it makes their world manageable and predictable. Most teens don't want to be class president, and they usually don't want to take on the role of parent. In the same way, most dogs are perfectly happy finding their niche in the family and have no desire to take on the responsibilities of leadership.

However, if no one takes the job of running the household, your child might have to. I know at least one family in which the parents have abdicated power to their daughter. The family is still intact, but no one is happy, least of all the teenage girl who would like to enjoy her youth. The same holds true with your dog, but having a canine at the head of your family can actually be dangerous. A dog thrust into the role of leader will almost always make the wrong decisions. He may decide that all mail carriers are terrorists and that his duty lies in chasing them (and other uniformed people) out of his territory. If the offending human doesn't leave, he may bite. This dog is leading his family and he has no idea how to do it. The position of head of household is an important one and should be taken on by someone who can handle it. Leadership, by the way, is not synonymous with dominance. A dog (or a person) can be very dominant without being leadership material. He may try to get his way by physically, verbally, or mentally bullying others, but that doesn't mean that he can properly handle problems or find needed resources.

What do leaders have to do? They have to make sure that there is enough food, water, and other supplies for the family. They have to make sure that the home is secure from unwanted intruders, and they're in charge of maintaining peace and cooperation in the home so that everything can proceed in the proper way. The rules

THE "DOG IN THE MANGER"

A client's dog was very much the "dog in the manger." Sebastian would grumble every time Marie even walked past him while he was resting. Although she had become frightened of him, she thought she should do something, so she'd tell him he was a very bad dog whenever he growled. Sebastian would just growl louder, and Marie would flinch, thus telling Sebastian he'd made an impact. As a result, Sebastian would get even more puffed up with himself. I suggested to Marie that she roll up his bed in the morning after he had been put outside to relieve himself. He had a lot of beds in the house and she took them all away. Then she started to hand-feed him, just as though he were a baby. She avoided situations that would provoke a growl and actively ignored him if he did something that displeased her. Instead of putting him on a tie-down or in another room—both actions that could provoke a growl—she would leave him in the room and exit herself or just go about her business as though he weren't there. It didn't take long for Sebastian to figure out that being nice to Marie was in his best interest, and their relationship got substantially better within a few weeks.

set up by a leader should be consistent within the family, and the dog should know what they are. When you raise an adolescent of either species, it's very unfair to them to make up new rules as you go along or even to make occasional exceptions to the rules. They need to know what to expect.

Convincing your adolescent child that you are the leader can be quite difficult at times, and so it is with adolescent dogs. Teenagers, at the cusp of adulthood, often want the best of both worlds. They want to make all their own decisions about where to go, what to buy, and whom to see at the same time they want you to drive them there, give them money, and facilitate them hanging out with their friends. Unfortunately for teens, parents do control all of the resources—the money, the transportation, and the home—or they should.

The essence of a successful parent-child or parent-dog relationship is not only controlling all of those things and making sure that she knows you control them, but it's also about convincing her that you're a fair and just parent. Does your teen

Many dog behaviors, such as chewing, are intrinsic, meaning they come naturally to a dog.

want to go to the movies? Then she must ask you, and you can decide whether it's appropriate for her to go. Does your dog want to visit with an oncoming dog? Then he should ask as well. Both dogs and teens should learn to ask, and a good parent will take their requests into consideration and comply when it seems reasonable.

MANAGING THE ENVIRONMENT

When we teach our children or our dogs, we should make sure that we set them up for success as much as possible. If your adolescent daughter tends to steal the car and take her friends out for joyrides every night, you might ground her for a time. That's punishment. You might also be wise to make the keys unavailable. That's management. If your dog tends to decimate your CD collection while you're at work, you'd be better off putting him in a place where he can't access the CDs or moving the CDs to a place where he can't get to them. If you really want him to learn to leave the CDs alone, you'll have to teach him, and for that you need to be there.

Managing your dog's environment may seem obvious, but often our preconceived notions of what dogs need or want interfere. Take this hypothetical case. Every day after Margie goes to work, her dog starts barking in the yard. The neighbors complain, and Margie has to come up with a solution fast. Because she believes that her dog needs to be outside "to play," she decides to stop the behavior by putting a shock collar on him so that he won't bark when she's gone. But he's already proven he's not ready to be outside on his own, and there's a good chance he's barking because he's anxious and overly reactive. The pain of the shock collar might decrease or eliminate the barking, but the anxiety won't go away and could actually increase. Other problems would be likely to pop up as well, like destruction or incessant whining. A humane and viable alternative to the collar would be for Margie to teach him to stay in a room in the house while she's at work, to make sure that he gets an adequate amount of exercise in the morning and evening, and to allow him to enjoy the yard when she's home. His anxiety will be reduced because the environment will not be so intimidating now. He's far less likely to bark, and if he does, he will be much more difficult to hear. (I should make it clear here that I do not use, recommend, or condone the use of shock collars or any other devices that use pain to modify behavior. Unfortunately, shock collars are getting more and more popular, and many people do use them to solve problems like barking.)

CONTROLLING THE STUFF OF LIFE

If you can approach, touch, and play with your dog any time you want and you have no behavior problems to deal with, your relationship is probably just fine the way it is. If your dog objects to any of your actions by growling, snarling, or running away, you have some work to do. The following are some benign ways to make sure that the family structure is appropriate.

Managing your dog's environment will help prevent him from getting into trouble.

Monitor Attention

Attention is very important in the world of a child or a dog—he who gets attention on demand is pretty powerful. How many of us have seen kids petulantly demanding that their parents pay attention to them now, when they want it, not when the parents have time to give it? We call those kids spoiled, and a dog who seeks and gets attention when he wants it is also spoiled. A spoiled dog will often nudge, push, and sometimes take his owner's arm into his mouth to get attention. Of course, neither the kid nor the dog is really "spoiled" in the true sense of the word. They are powerful, and they know how to use their power to get what they want.

To relieve your dog of this inappropriate power, your job is to monitor and control the amount of attention you pay to him and to make sure that you initiate most interactions. You can occasionally ignore him when he seeks petting and occasionally give him attention when he doesn't want it. Sometimes you can ask him to "say please" when he would like your attention, perhaps by sitting first.

Attention goes hand in hand with other resources, food being a primary one. You can show your dog who is the "great hunter" by hand-feeding him sometimes, especially the good stuff. Another idea is to hang around his food dish when he's eating—not to interrupt him, not to take food out of it (how rude!), but to be present and to occasionally add a little bit to it.

Control the Territory

Teens love their space—their exclusive territory. They usually want to decorate their rooms in their own particular style, and they often hang out in there for hours. Sometimes they're sleeping, listening to music, talking on the phone, or surfing the Web. Some teens hang signs on their doors indicating that you, as an adult, are not welcome. Adolescent dogs also love their space—their bed or their favorite corner. Some dogs will growl or snap if you try to move them, and some dogs will take your bed as their own if they can. Many a spouse has been startled to be kicked out of bed by the dog who laid claim to the best resting place by taking advantage of a bathroom break.

Controlling this resource should be done before problems develop. Deciding where your dog sleeps and whether he can get on your bed are decisions you need to make in the beginning of your relationship, not when he's confronting you. You can always relax the rules later when he's earned your trust and you've earned his. If your dog does challenge you, your best response is likely to be no response at all: no eye contact, no threat back, nothing. In effect, you are telling him that you are so powerful that his challenge is beneath your notice, just as it would be if a child threatened you. Instead, take action of a different sort. Take advantage of the fact that he's a family animal, and mentally kick him out of the family for a few days. Ignore him most of the time, and pay him no attention whatsoever when he approaches you for attention. When you feed him, make sure that he's very polite, sitting for each mouthful. You'll need to exercise him, but you don't have to interact when

Dogs can be territorial when it comes to doorways, a behavior that requires you to take action.

you do. Give him the cold shoulder for a couple of days and then cheerfully resume your normal life. In addition, manage his environment by making sure that he's not in a position where he feels a growl is called for. That could mean moving his bed or having him sleep in a crate. It could also mean having him drag a short leash around the house for a couple of weeks as a reminder of who controls what.

I've mentioned that doorways can be extremely important to many dogs, who will do everything they can to be first out the door. In fact, doorways are where many "sibling" fights occur, as two dogs vie for the door and thus run into each other. In addition, some dogs will guard the top of a staircase, gaining status and stature by looking down at their human. These are all permutations of territoriality, and if your dog does these things, you should consider taking some action. You

The Dangers of Inactivity

One of my clients was a nice young couple that had bought an Australian Blue Heeler puppy because they liked the way he looked. During puppy classes, the youngster was just great. Heelers tend to be very intelligent, and Buddy was no exception; he learned *sit*, *down*, *stay*, and *come* in record time, and his owners were justifiably proud of themselves and him. They took him for hikes every day and enjoyed his company immensely. Unfortunately, at six months of age, Buddy was diagnosed with hip dysplasia. Their veterinarian recommended surgery to replace one hip, and the owners decided to go ahead with it. The surgery went fine, and Buddy began to recuperate. For the hip to set properly, though, Buddy had to remain quiet for about two months. That's when the problems began. The owners tried very hard—they exercised his mind by teaching him tricks, and they gave him lots of attention. Unfortunately, his behavior got worse and worse, and they had to go to work (to pay for his surgery!). Every day he'd get into trouble. If they left him in a crate, he barked and cried for hours; if they didn't, he'd destroy something in the house.

One day I was walking through our shelter and I saw a familiar figure sitting in the lobby looking intelligent and interested—Buddy. Next to him was his mom, crying. Buddy had destroyed her husband's briefcase, which contained some very valuable papers, and that had done it. They didn't feel they could keep him anymore. Luckily, this story has a happy ending. My family fostered the pup until his hip was healed, and then we found him a new owner—a trainer who could give Buddy all the stimulation he needed. I see him around from time to time; he still gives his owner a run for her money, but she's up to it.

If Buddy had not had the surgery, would his owners have kept him? In all likelihood, yes. His exploratory tendencies were exacerbated greatly by his physical inaction, and his owners didn't have the time, expertise, or the patience to cope. At the height of his adolescence, Buddy was forced to go without exercise, and it just didn't work.

could control the staircase scenario by not letting him upstairs or by cheerfully calling him down whenever he perches up there. My German Shepherd, Strider, is a confirmed door charger. As a result, he has to lie down when I open the door, go through only when I allow it, and then lie down again once he's outside.

Prevent Food and Toy Possessiveness

Some dogs figure that what's theirs is theirs and what's yours is theirs, and they will guard any food or toys that come their way. Again, this behavior can be seen all over the human world. We all love our "stuff." Earlier, I discussed several ways of handling possessive behavior, but if your dog has made it to adolescence and is still guarding food or toys, you'll need to work even harder to fix the behavior. (I will discuss some techniques later.)

Some dogs also throw tantrums, the equivalent of charging into their rooms and slamming the door. When they display this behavior, it's usually because they're frustrated and they're trying to control you. The best example of this is something called "leash aggression." The proper term is more likely "leash frustration," as it's really not aggression. It's the dog feeling furious that you're holding him back from something he wants—usually to play with another dog. Most dogs with this problem tend to pull on their leashes when they're being walked and are already in a state of excitement, so the sight of another dog can send them into a frenzy. (I'll have more on this problem behavior later as well.)

THE NEED FOR STIMULATION

Adolescents need stimulation as well as structure, and lots of it. If our teenagers are involved in after-school activities of some kind or another, they're far less likely to explore the seedier side of life. The same is true with dogs. Any kind of constructive activity, whether it be physical or mental, will have numerous positive effects on your adolescent dog.

Exercise

One of the best activities is one involving large muscle movement—exercise. Dogs who are sufficiently exercised follow the same pattern; in fact, a good adolescent is an exhausted adolescent—of either species! Without exercise, both can get into massive amounts of trouble and try your patience to the core.

Confident adolescent dogs tend to be social and want to meet other dogs.

Because of the society we live in, giving a dog enough exercise can be difficult. Walking 20 minutes in the morning and evening may be enough for an eight-year-old dog, but it definitely isn't enough for an adolescent. He needs substantial exercise at least twice a day, playing ball or going for athletic walks or hikes. Often, joggers or runners want their dog to be an exercise companion. This is a great idea, but you should check with your vet to find out when your dog is sufficiently mature enough to run steadily for miles (km) without straining his joints too much. Exercise is one area where small dog owners have it easy. Little dogs are much easier to exercise, especially if they play fetch. They can even be exercised inside the house.

I recommend both morning and evening exercise because dogs are naturally the most active during these times of day, and you can encourage that tendency with a consistent and predictable routine. Your dog will tend to rest after exercise, which is very helpful if you have a daytime job.

Mental Stimulation

Besides their physical needs, adolescent dogs need mental stimulation. Most breeds of dogs used to have real jobs; Heelers, for instance, are still used to herd cattle. Put an intelligent animal in a backyard with nothing to do, though, and he'll find something with which to amuse himself. He might dig or teach himself how to garden. He might re-landscape your yard in ways you never envisioned, or he might bark at every tiny movement he hears—and he can hear a lot!

Mental stimulation can come in the form of training, exercise conducted in a variety of places, or games. There are lots of great games for inquiring minds. For instance, you can teach your dog to find toys in your house or yard, or you can lengthen mealtime by stuffing a treat dispenser with kibble. For the more ambitious, tricks like "shake" or "roll over" are fairly simple to teach and can wear a dog out quickly.

Interaction With Other Dogs

One way to fill many needs is to have your dog play with other dogs. Proper socialization is lots of fun and is also a good method for both dogs and their owners to meet other people. Dog parks are gaining in popularity around the country, and many people visit them daily. Dog parks can be wonderful tools, but they can also be dangerous territory, depending on who is populating them at any given time. I mentioned earlier that it's our job as parents to monitor our dog's friends. I don't want my daughter to socialize with kids who do drugs, drink, or don't care about school, and I don't want my dog to socialize with the undesirable elements of the canine world, either.

Confident adolescent dogs tend to be pretty social. They usually want to meet other dogs, and they do it enthusiastically. Shy adolescents, on the other hand, often don't want to meet other dogs. Many adult dogs either don't like adolescents in their faces, or they don't like to play with other dogs at all unless they know them well. Because we take pups from their own species at eight weeks, some dogs never learn from their real mothers how to meet and greet other dogs. Thus, it falls to us human parents to teach them.

Your dog's first few experiences at a dog park or other social gathering are extremely important. If he's attacked or even hit accidentally by another dog, he won't easily forget it. Thus, you should be very careful. A popular dog park can be like a popular playground or soccer field—the fun can go out of control quickly, and then someone will get hurt. It needs "yard monitors," and often dog owners don't see themselves as such. Many people tend to stand in one area, letting the dogs play with abandon. However, it's our responsibility to watch our dogs, to learn to recognize canine body language, and to stop problems before they become serious.

Cautious Greetings

Our old Rottweiler, Jobear, introduced himself to other dogs very well indeed; he was wonderful to watch. He'd see another dog, slow down, look slightly away and then back, walk toward the other dog in an arc, approach carefully, sniff at the other dog's chin, then around the back, and then either play or leave. He gave out "nice" vibes and never got into any kind of fight, although he was attacked once. He seemed astounded at the attack, which ended quickly with no injury to him. However, for the rest of his life, Jobear never really completely trusted me to keep him safe. When other dogs approached, he would avoid them politely, walk about 200 feet (61 m) up the road, and wait for me and the other dogs to catch up.

Dogs interacting with other dogs can be delightful and educational to watch, and I urge you to do so. You can see dogs "talking" to each other—inviting each other to play or telling them to go away. Adolescents who haven't learned the nuances of canine communication are usually pretty insensitive. They greet other dogs as though they've known them for months, sometimes ramming into them, sometimes trying to mount them. And they're astounded when another dog snaps at them to make them go away.

Recognizing Play

Recognizing play can be difficult at times, but with practice you can get quite good at it. Generally speaking, dogs who are playing change their "roles" quite often, and their play is fairly jerky, with short freezes. Thus, one dog might be on top of another, and then suddenly the second dog is on top. One dog might be chasing another dog and quickly turn to be chased. Often, play will be accompanied by "play bows," where one or both dogs will stretch out their forelegs, drop their front ends, and raise their hind ends. Some dogs play very noisily, while others are quiet. Some breeds or breed types play very differently from one another. For example, German Shepherds tend to growl and bark a lot; Boxers use their front paws and jump on top of other dogs; and Labs often ram into their playmates. Problems can arise if two dogs have incompatible play styles and have trouble communicating with each other. For instance, a noisy German Shepherd could terrify a shy Shetland Sheepdog, or a fun-loving Labrador could easily offend a mature and dignified Rottweiler. Sometimes one dog will growl or snap at another to tell the dog to back off. When that happens, many humans think the snapping dog is the aggressor. This could be the case, but often it isn't.

Greeting Rituals

Imagine a complete stranger walking up to you and giving you a hug. Would you laugh and tell him he's wonderful? Of course not. We humans have greeting rituals, like quick eye contact, shaking hands, or just saying hello. We give each other space before initiating an intimate involvement. The same is true with dogs, where the technique should be to approach each other politely and slowly and then ask to play.

It's a popular myth that dogs are always trying to dominate each other. If dogs know each other—even for a few minutes—they may attempt to figure out who's stronger and smarter. However, body slamming and mounting are usually just plain rude!

Bullying

Some dogs experiment with their power, but their behavior might be better described as bullying. Ananda was a very good example of a bully dog. She was a German Shepherd Dog who was surrendered to the shelter where I work when she was about ten months old. She had an overpowering personality— friendly, outgoing, and highly physical. When we let her play with other dogs, she introduced herself by racing right up to them and throwing herself at their shoulders. She did the same to people, leaping up and landing squarely on their chests. She could easily knock over

Some dogs experiment with their power, even going so far as to bully another dog.

a child or a fragile adult. She was the epitome of rude behavior—the result of no structure in her first home, combined with a forceful personality. A few adult dogs could handle her—those who knew how to deliver a quick reprimand. When she was introduced to an adult German Shorthaired Pointer mix, he did a masterful job of putting her in her place. He froze, stared, growled, and waited. Ananda played around a little bit, then decided that discretion was the better part of valor and went off to find another victim. (She chose a human in that session.) We worked on Ananda for weeks, trying to teach her the good manners she'd missed in the first few months of her life, and she picked up obedience beautifully. She would sit, lie down, stay, and walk politely on the leash. But as soon as she was released to play, she'd revert to her previous behavior. Eventually she was adopted, but after three months her owner gave up and returned her. She was just too exhausting.

Keeping this story in mind, I suggest that you socialize your dog to other dogs, but very carefully. Dogs should learn to introduce themselves politely and to play differently with different dogs so they can move effortlessly from one situation to another. One traumatic experience can shape your dog's attitude toward other dogs forever. If he's being bullied at a dog park, you should leave immediately. If he begins to be a bully—jumping on top of other dogs or chasing them—you should

Your dog should be carefully socialized to other dogs.

CHECKLIST

- ❖ Integrate a new adolescent into your home by setting clear, firm rules, at least for several months. You should control the territory, the food, the amount of attention your dog gets, and where he sleeps. After several months, the rules can be relaxed a bit.

- ❖ Make sure that your dog gets enough physical and mental exercise: walks, runs, or play periods twice a day at minimum, as well as training sessions or games.

- ❖ Expect your adolescent to be very curious and possibly very destructive, and take steps to minimize any damage. He will grow out of it.

- ❖ Keep your dog as safe as you can from any traumatic incidents that might influence future behavior. Check out play partners and play areas carefully.

only allow him to play with dogs who can handle that behavior; even then, don't let the fun get out of hand. If you think that your dog is uncomfortable, frightened, or acting inappropriately, take action. Put yourself firmly in your parental shoes, and manage the environment as much as you can. If you can't, leave. Don't expect other owners to take action with their dogs. There's a good chance they don't see any problems, and you'll just end up in an unpleasant altercation.

Chapter Eight

House Manners

Many people would be happy just to have a civilized dog: a dog who doesn't pee on the furniture or chew it up, beg at the table at mealtimes, cry, whine, or bark when left alone in the house, steal food from the counter, or bite anyone. Civilized behavior can be taught (really!) with patience and persistence. There are those who believe that formal "obedience" training will solve all of their dog's behavior issues. Alas, this is not so. Obedience will certainly help solve some problems, but not all of them. It especially won't help with indoor behavior. That's up to you and your good sense. In this section, we will be using some formal exercises but teaching them in the context of house manners, which is probably a better way to teach them anyway.

GETTING STARTED

First and foremost, you need to remember that as the parent, you must take time to teach. This is very important. Often we assume that our dogs automatically know not to rummage through the garbage can, chew our socks, drink out of the toilet, or eat the wall, but they don't. By managing the environment and by discouraging the offending behavior, you will make far more headway than by catching him in the act and punishing him for it. Trading your sock for his cookie is a good way to teach your dog to bring things to you and to give them up readily. If he has his paws on the kitchen counter, going into the kitchen and moving his paws so that he has to get off is much more effective than yelling at him from afar. We human beings love to use our voices to express our displeasure, but action is so much more powerful than words.

The Crate

Let's assume that you're bringing home an adolescent and you'd like to start right. The first thing to do is buy a crate. I can think of no reason for not teaching your dog to stay in a crate. If it is done correctly, he'll think of the crate as his little territory, a place he can go to relax, just as your teen's room might be (minus the loud music). At first, you can use the crate to aid in housetraining and management when you can't keep an eye on him. (Refer to the crate-training methods described in Chapter 2.) Once your dog is reliable, you can put the crate away, although you may wish to keep it for future situations—for instance, when you go on a trip and want to take him with you, when you have some uncivilized little humans over to play, or when he's very dirty and you have to wait a few minutes to clean him.

CASE STUDY

GOING FOR A WALK

You can teach your dog to calm down before going for a walk. You don't need a partner, just patience. The first dog with whom I ever went through this process was our Rottweiler, Barney. Whenever I picked up his leash to go for a walk, he would get very enthusiastic. In fact, his jumping up and down could shake the whole house. I finally convinced him that he wasn't going anywhere without being calm. First, I picked up his leash. He started his hysterical act. I then said "Oops" and sat down on a kitchen chair a few feet (m) from the door. After a few seconds, he looked at me in obvious confusion, calmed down a bit, and then finally sat. I got up, he jumped up, I sat down, he sat down. In about three minutes, after about 50 repetitions, I stood up and he stayed in his *sit*. Then I started to open the door. Barney leaped up. I sat down. It took him only ten or so repetitions for this to work, and from there we were out the door and on our walk. His pace, by the way, was quite amusing to watch. Each step was obviously inhibited. He really wanted to let loose but knew that he couldn't.

The Tie-Down

You'll also need a good, strong, short leash, preferably made out of bicycle chain. This is called a tie-down or tether, and it also is a great management tool for limiting your dog's movement when you're not watching him. The tie-down should be attached to an immovable object or an eyebolt in the wall, and it should be located right next to a nice blanket or dog bed. You can use a tie-down for time-outs or just as managed resting spots. It's a wonderful tool for having your dog close to you without needing to watch him every second. Most dogs get used to it quickly, just as a young child can get used to a playpen. (This is one of the very wonderful things about your dog *not* being a human teenager. I can't imagine a 15-year-old putting up with being kept in a location of your choice!)

If your dog is unreliable in the house, then it's up to you to keep an eye on him. Your presence should have a dampening effect on his urge to experiment. If it doesn't, you can give yourself an edge by attaching a 4-foot (1-m) leash to him and leaving it on in the house. If he suddenly gets an urge for a "puppy rush" (flying

If you never reinforce begging behavior, it is less likely to occur.

around the house at 90 miles [145 km] an hour, crashing into everything that's in his way), you'll have a tool to slow him down. If he grabs a pair of glasses and you don't yet have confidence that trading for a treat will work, you can step on the leash and gently extract the glasses.

TABLE MANNERS

Once you have your management tools at the ready, you'll want to decide what constitutes good manners. You might want to teach your dog to sit politely for his dinner, for instance.[1] It's actually quite easy, as long as you are consistent. Hold the bowl of food above his head. When he sits, start to put the bowl down. If he gets up (which he will), pull the bowl back up. Your goal is to have him maintain a solid *sit* until the bowl reaches the floor. Then you can tell him he can have it. Sometimes you'll need to give him a tidbit from the bowl while he is sitting to keep him from getting overly frustrated.

Be aware that if someone in your household gives your dog food from the table "just this once because he looks so cute," your dog is likely to think that hovering near the table will eventually lead to more food. What's more, he's probably right! It's a solid scientific fact that behaviors that are randomly reinforced (those occasional scraps from the table) are more difficult to eliminate than ones that are reinforced every time and then stopped. In fact, random reinforcement actually makes a behavior stronger.

Teens are a good example of this phenomenon. If you give your teenage daughter an allowance, she'll probably learn that she'd better spend wisely, and she's not likely to bug you for more money, except in an emergency. (Of course, it's her definition

[1] A recent study showed that just teaching a dog to sit before anything he wants caused most people to like their dogs more—and to keep them longer

of an emergency, not yours.) If, on the other hand, you occasionally give in when she asks for extra money, she's likely to keep asking, even if you say no most of the time. Her requests may also increase in intensity if she knows from experience that persistence pays off at least some of the time.

That's what we call random reinforcement. It's powerful stuff and is much better used for behaviors you like and want rather than those you would like to discourage.

GREETING MANNERS

Good greeting behavior can be much more difficult than good meal manners. Unlike people, most dogs have to go through a greeting ritual with everyone, even if they've only been gone minutes. This is one of those intrinsic behaviors discussed earlier. Some dogs want to jump up and lick your lips (a submissive gesture); others try to barrel you over roughly (definitely not submissive). The fact that we stop actually invites the dog to jump up, and when we push them away with our hands, it's an invitation to play harder. If you don't want your dog jumping on you, practice completely ignoring him for three minutes or so after you come home. Better yet, walk through the house into a back room and get busy with something. By the time you actually greet your dog, you'll be old hat. Of course, most people want their dogs to greet them (sometimes the dog is the only member of the family who's glad you came home) and actually encourage excited greetings.

The Ignoring Game

If your dog greets you enthusiastically, chances are he'll do the same for your guests. The ignoring game will generally work for friends, but sometimes they're not as comfortable just walking into your house after you've opened the door. If you want to try it, tell them in advance what you'd like them to do. When you open the door, they should walk all the way into the house to a designated spot, open a cookie jar, ask your dog to sit, and give him a treat or two.

Using Treats

An alternative method of discouraging rough greetings is to place a bowl of small crispy treats right outside the door. When your guest comes in, she should

Your adolescent dog should learn good greeting behavior.

scatter some of the little treats on the floor, purposely allowing a few to hit the dog on the head so that he is distracted from his greeting. Most dogs will get busy looking for the food and will forget all about greeting. After a while they'll expect the treats and will make do with one from the hand. Eventually—when the behavior is very reliable—you can occasionally reinforce with treats.

Teaching *Sit*

If you start early and only have one dog, it's quite possible to teach him to sit for your guests. You should practice at any door through which your guests might arrive. Begin by teaching him to stay in a *sit* when the door is opened. At first, you and your family members will be the "guests" who come through the door.

1. Ask your dog to sit about 10 feet (3 m) away from the door, far enough that it can open without banging into him. Stand next to him, holding his leash.
2. When he's in place, encourage a family member or friend to open the door.
3. If he stands up, say "Oops" or "Too bad" or something equally condescending, and close the door.
4. Ask him to sit again in the same place, and go through the same process. He needs to stay sitting the entire time the door is opening and until the "guest" is inside.
5. Lavishly reward him while he is still sitting. Make sure that you give him his treats at *sit* level so that he doesn't feel the need to jump for them.

   If you have a very enthusiastic dog, you might even drop a few treats on the ground after you release him to discourage jumping up. Ideally, you should reach a point where you don't have to give him a verbal cue at all. He should just go to the door, sit, and wait for the reward.

Reinforcing Calm Behavior

Another method of discouraging overly enthusiastic greetings is to make the behavior appear to drive away the guest.

1. Ask your guest to knock on the door and begin to open it.
2. When your dog leaps up to greet your guest, say "Off" and tell your guest to close the door without coming in.
3. Practice this several times with different guests until the dog learns that people won't come in until he's calm.

Alternatively, you can use the "Stupid Mom Routine" I described in Chapter 4.

1. Leave a leash on your dog but let it drag.
2. When he jumps up, ask him cheerfully if he wants to go outside, then pick up the leash and take him out the door.
3. Then stay in the house and leave him outside for five seconds.
4. Bring him back in cheerfully, and be prepared to do it a few more times.

After a few repetitions, he's likely to give up completely, probably thinking you are one of the densest humans on the planet!

There are more aversive ways to discourage jumping up. These methods can work but usually only for the individual doing the punishing and not necessarily for visitors who might feel uncomfortable hurting or spraying your dog with water. Expecting your guests to time the punishment correctly may also be unrealistic. Thus, your dog may end up feeling that you're pretty dangerous, but everyone else is just fine. It's much better to find alternative, more positive behaviors that work for everyone.

It's very difficult for most of us to keep the rules we set up for a dog. But giving in—even "just this once"—leads to confusion, and a confused dog is not usually what we think of as a good dog.

WHAT YOU SAY, WHAT YOU MEAN, AND WHAT THEY HEAR

When I say to my daughter "Did you finish your homework?" I really mean "Why are you sitting there watching television when you should be doing something productive?" My daughter hears "You don't trust me to finish my homework on my own." I'm a parent talking to my teenage daughter, a member of my family for 16 years, and we are not really communicating. Imagine what your dog hears when

Prevent communication problems with your dog by saying a command only once—don't repeat it over and over.

you say something to him! (I'm very glad this book isn't trying to address the hidden messages in human communication. It's so much more complex than communicating with dogs.)

The nuances of speech—tone, volume, and emotion—are many and varied in the human world. Patricia McConnell has written about this at length in her excellent book *The Other End of the Leash*. The dog hears all of the variables, and there's a good chance he's confused by them. Even a simple cue like *come* can have a whole host of meanings: "come to dinner," "come home from playing," "come here right now."

I taught my dog, Strider, to lie down on the cue "Lie down." I taught my Belgian Tervuren, Ariel, to perform the same behavior on the word "down." If I say "Down" to Strider, he looks confused and he doesn't lie down. To him, the word that asks for the behavior is probably something like "lydown"—it is one word and has a very specific meaning. If I say "Lie down" to Ariel, she looks at me in confusion. I have some clients who say "Sit down" to their dogs, but these animals then don't know whether to sit or to lie down. In addition, the word "down" is often used for "get off my body" or "get off the counter."

One of our most common communication problems is repeating our cues over and over again. Sometimes a dog will figure that he's supposed to wait until the complete cue is given: "downdowndownDOWN." I find myself doing it: "Sit. I said sit!" And I'm sure that my dogs think I have two cues for most exercises. There's "come." And then there's "come NOW." We need to clean up our language to communicate better.

When you're teaching your dog, I suggest that you choose a vocabulary and then

stick with it as much as possible. When using a verbal cue, try to make the emphasis the same. For instance, if you're impatient or frustrated, try not to sound like it. Many trainers use a device called a clicker when teaching their dogs. The device always sounds the same and can help dogs learn more quickly. It's hard for a click to sound angry!

Words, though, aren't the only method of communicating with our dogs; body language is even more powerful. Unfortunately, we often aren't aware of the physical signals we are giving. If you tower over your dog, he may cower or back up. If you squat and clap your hands, he's likely to move toward you. If you stare at him, he might feel threatened. Like kids, dogs and their reactions differ from one individual to another. If you take the time to observe your dog, you may find it interesting and entertaining to see what his responses are to your body language cues.

Chapter Nine

Learning Basics and Dog Behavior

Classroom teachers usually take quite some time at the beginning of a school year to establish a working relationship with their students. They set up a calm learning environment, which paves the way for their children to succeed. The children, in turn, know what is expected of them and what will happen if they transgress. Good teachers take as much time as necessary to teach a particular skill. The same basic principles that apply to children and teachers in a classroom should also apply to you, the teacher, and your dog, the student. For example, the environment in which you teach your dog should be calm and under your control. In addition, you shouldn't start a lesson if you're angry or upset, and you should stop teaching immediately if you do lose your temper. Good teachers make for good students.

The best kind of learning is the kind kids want to do. A teen may be horrible at algebra but know how to set up and run a computer beautifully. Or a teen may have trouble with spelling but have a wonderful aptitude for art. Each child has talents of her own, and when that child is learning how to use them, she may acquire knowledge and skill very quickly. My daughter has an exhaustive store of knowledge about music and art, for instance. However, subjects that don't interest her are much more difficult for her to learn. Often, teaching these subjects requires a great deal of work on the parts of both the teacher and the student.

The behaviors that dogs can learn easily tend to have had value before domestication. For example, once a dog has learned to steal food from the garbage, dig holes, or chase cats, it can be very difficult to stop these activities. That's because these behaviors are hardwired—once introduced, the dog learns them quickly. They are also naturally reinforced; the behavior itself is so much fun that no other reward is required.

It's more difficult for dogs to learn and to retain behaviors that go against their nature. In fact, even after you have taught your dog to perform certain exercises well, he may have a tendency to forget them over a period of months or years. This too has its human equivalent. Say your daughter has a hard time learning algebra, but she manages to pass the courses that are required. Because the subject was difficult and math not her natural bent, there's a good chance the knowledge will only last as long as it has to and not carry through to adulthood.

This tendency to forget certain behaviors means that you'll have to practice them more than others, and you'll have to reward them more often. For dogs, the behaviors include many normal obedience exercises, especially the *come*.

CONSEQUENCES

Each behavior that is performed by a person or a dog has a consequence. Some of these are natural consequences and some are ones that we supply. We tend to repeat behaviors that have a positive consequence, like reading for enjoyment or eating to feel satisfied. We do not repeat behaviors that have negative consequences; touching a hot stove, for example, is not something people do often, at least on purpose! When you're teaching, it's your job to supply the consequences to help your student learn what you wish him to do.

Positive Consequences

Dogs, like teenagers, need to feel there's a reason for doing something dull or uninteresting. If they don't find the reason compelling, they will expect some sort of

Behaviors such as digging through the garbage can be difficult to stop because they are naturally reinforcing.

POSSESSION ISSUES

One of my more memorable consults involved an elderly couple—let's call them John and Lily—and their adolescent Rottweiler, Max. Max was very strong; neither owner could actually walk him without being dragged, but that wasn't the real problem. Max had possession issues. He loved his own toys, bones, and food, but he also loved John and Lily's stuff. While I was in their house, Max took hand towels from the towel rack, a pipe filled with tobacco, several socks, a vase, and three or four books—all within the space of 30 minutes or so. When the couple tried to remove the items from Max's mouth, he would growl and snap, and at 100+ pounds (45.5+ kg), the growl was pretty intimidating. I asked them what they'd been doing about it, and John said that every time he caught Max, he'd take him by his jowls, shake him, and throw him on the floor! I was astounded that he could even do this and even more astounded that Max let him. John was very proud of his punishment technique until I asked him how that was working for him. After a few seconds of hard thought, he admitted that it wasn't working at all. It didn't meet the criteria for effective punishment, and it was downright dangerous to John as well. We agreed on a management plan involving space control, obedience work, and some friendly trading practices to modify the behavior. The combination worked quite well, although I'm still not at all sure that Max was the right dog for that couple.

reward for doing it. Humans, of course, can understand the concept of a delayed reward. For your teen, it might be "Finish your homework and you can go out." A dog doesn't have the capacity to anticipate a distant reward, as in "If you don't dig holes while I'm gone, I'll take you for a walk later." (Wouldn't it be great if they did? Many problems could be instantly solved.) Thus, for a dog, the reward must follow the behavior quickly or the dog won't understand the connection between the two. This should be the driving force for all of your teaching and will help you every time you get frustrated with your dog.

Positive consequences must be rewarding to the person or animal getting rewarded! Your teenage daughter might appreciate praise for keeping her room clean, but she'd really like a few perks, like a later curfew for the weekend. Most dogs couldn't care less about a pat on the head and a hearty "Good dog." It's not really very rewarding. A delicious treat is rewarding, and many dogs will work for that. The reward should also be generous. If you were to extend the curfew for your teenager, you wouldn't do it for just ten minutes—it would be more like an hour. When it comes to dog training, we humans tend to be cheap. We sometimes have a hard time parting with even the smallest, most inexpensive treats. Practice generosity—it's very effective, and you'll be pleased with the results.

A delicious treat to reward a desired action is an example of a positive consequence.

Negative Consequences

If your dog is doing something wrong and you'd like to stop it, you have several choices. First, of course, is prevention. If that's not possible, there are a couple of kinds of negative consequences at your disposal.

Time-Outs and Loss of Privileges

Little kids usually want to be with other people (mostly Mom), so short bursts of isolation, like time-outs, are often very effective at correcting unwanted behavior. However, as your child gets older, she may actually want to be alone, in which case isolation is completely ineffective unless it's accompanied by something she dislikes (cleaning her room, for instance). This is true for dogs too. A time-out for a puppy can be effective as long as it's quite short (30 seconds to 2 minutes), whereas for an adolescent, it's often an invitation to get into things unless the environment is under your control.

The "Stupid Mom Routine" is actually controlled isolation and works well for both puppies and adolescents. During this routine, you will give your dog a time-out when he's doing something you don't want by putting him outside with his leash on while you hold the end of the leash inside for several seconds. The time-out works because he's isolated, but his environment is being controlled because he's on leash and cannot do what he would like.

A common way to indicate your displeasure to your teenager is to take away privileges, like going out in the evening or driving the car. You can take comparable action with an adolescent dog by not giving him something that he fully expects to have. Of course, your dog should actually see what he's losing because he doesn't think in abstract terms. You'll see this used when you teach the *stay*. I also use it when practicing *recalls* (*come*). I place a treat on the ground, and the owner calls her dog, who has to run past the treat to get to the owner. If the dog stops at the treat, it's covered up before he can get to it. If the dog runs past the treat to the owner, he gets a reward when he arrives. The dog is then escorted back to the treat he passed and is given that as well (lots of positive reinforcement!).

Many people think that punishment will eliminate a behavior, but generally it just suppresses the behavior.

Punishment

Many people think that by punishing their dog, they'll eliminate a behavior.

Actually, punishment generally just suppresses behavior. If my dog is jumping up on me and I physically punish him, he will stop the practice. However, while my dog may stop jumping on me, he'll most likely continue to jump on other people. If you punish a dog for counter surfing by yelling at him, the behavior will be suppressed when you're in the room but will pop right back out when you're elsewhere. (Then when you come back in, your dog will look "guilty.") To punish your dog and have it stick, you have to meet several criteria. This is extraordinarily difficult, which is one reason why I don't use this technique often. (The other reason is that I've made a choice not to.) The following are some criteria you have to meet for punishment to be effective.

❖ **The punishment must be the appropriate strength.** The punishment will make a big impression on the dog, meaning he'll remember it well enough not to repeat the behavior. This is very difficult because we don't know what a dog considers big or memorable. Some dogs are pretty resilient, while others are very sensitive. And in the case of physical punishment, some dogs will fight back. If the punishment is not big enough, it will backfire, and you will have to escalate the punishment to be effective. On the other hand, a minor punishment for a major crime is often counterproductive.

❖ **Your timing must be impeccable.** The punishment must be attached to the event in the dog's mind. This is also extremely difficult. Because we don't know what goes on in the dog's mind, it's quite possible that we're punishing the wrong event—something that occurred after the original misdeed. Instead of punishing the dog for jumping on the counter, for instance, you could be punishing him for sitting afterward.

Similarly, say you push your dog off the counter every time he jumps up on it. Then you ask for a *sit* and reward him for that particular action. If your timing isn't exactly right, you might actually reward him for jumping up, and the fact that you pushed him won't matter much.

❖ **Punishment should come from the environment, not from your hands.** If your dog steals food from the counter and you strike him, he may not jump on the counter anymore, but he may also be afraid of you or your hands. Many people have observed dogs who cringe when someone raises an arm. Most likely, these dogs have been punished and see people as dangerous. A better choice for your counter jumper might be a booby trap set up in advance. For example, you might put some food on a baking tray so that when your dog's feet touch the tray, it'll fall on him. You don't have to be in sight when this occurs, although you should probably be in the vicinity to make sure that he doesn't end up eating the food that's now on the floor.

❖ **It should happen every time the misbehavior occurs.** Yes, even when you're in the shower or not at home. Sometimes this one is downright impossible.

❖ **If it hasn't worked after three to four attempts, stop.** It's a human tendency to keep trying, even when a punishment has yet to be successful. A common example is just the word "no." It's very common for people to yell "No!" at their dog when he's barking, even though it often makes the problem worse. Many people will just shout louder and louder, hoping that at some point their shouting will achieve results.

❖ **Your dog has to care about you.** Shortly after adopting Strider, my two-year-old

German Shepherd, I identified a couple of serious problem behaviors we'd have to work on. He barked in the car when other dogs walked by, and he often lunged at the end of the leash when in the presence of other dogs. (He looked pretty fierce!) My first attempts at modifying those behaviors were unsuccessful because I had no relationship with Strider. He didn't know me and had no reason to trust or care about me. However, after he'd been part of my family for five months or so, the same behavior modification methods worked very well and the problems diminished and then disappeared. Our relationship had improved and so had his desire to please me.

CHECKLIST

❖ Remember that dogs can easily learn behaviors that would be part of their natural heritage; exercises that inhibit behavior or are unnatural take much longer and will need more practice and more reinforcement.

❖ The reinforcement you use should be reinforcing to the dog. Although we think that kibble should work, the dog may not. Many a client has told me that her dog won't work for food when he will—as soon as the right food is found.

❖ Use punishment sparingly because it doesn't usually get rid of behaviors. Most of the time, the dog will just wait until you are gone to repeat them. If you do punish, make sure that the punishment is appropriate, of the right strength, and won't damage your relationship.

Why do humans want to punish? Sometimes people use punishment because they are angry or frustrated. Sometimes it's because other people witness the problem behavior, and they expect you to punish your dog. At any rate, over the years I've found that catching your dog doing something right is much more fun and much more effective than waiting to correct your dog when he does something wrong.

Chapter Ten

Formal Training Preparation

By the time your child goes to junior high school, she already knows some basics. Presumably, she knows how to share, how to say please, and not to run out into the street. The same goes for your dog because you've been doing informal training since you got him. Now it's time to advance to more complicated lessons. The exercises outlined in the following sections will help both of you learn to communicate clearly in a language you will both understand. If you've been working on what I've described in the preceding sections, you should find this stuff quite easy.

BASIC SUPPLIES

You'll need to make sure that you have equipped yourself with everything you need to be a good teacher. For you, that's an optimistic attitude, and for your student, it's something to keep him interested in learning. As mentioned earlier, that something is usually food—good food. Although some lucky teachers have dogs who love to work, most would rather be chasing rabbits. Make sure that the food you plan to use

Things like toys and balls can provide positive reinforcement for your dog.

is food your dog loves. His normal dinner food, like kibble, is not usually enticing enough. I suggest offering small bits of soft nutritious food. You're going to be generous with your rewards, so you may as well make sure that he doesn't fill up on the equivalent of hamburgers and fries. And of course, he should be hungry when you train him.

Toys, balls, and activities can also provide reinforcement for your dog. They can be very powerful with some dogs and deserve attention and exploration. Some dogs love to chase a ball or play tug-of-war as a reward, while some like to wrestle for a few seconds. These rewards will come in handy as you and your dog move from grade school to high school to college. However, in the beginning stages, treats will be more effective because of the speed of reinforcement.

If you're using food, you'll need a reward bag. Commonly called a "bait" or "treat" bag, it holds the treats to give your dog when he does something right. It's extremely important to have one, although the look can be quite unfashionable. Old fanny packs are fine, or you can buy a bag at a pet shop. Use something that attaches to your clothing or that can be tied around your waist and will leave your hands free. It should be easily accessible—you don't want to be fishing deep into your pockets for a treat for five minutes after your dog just performed exquisitely!

WHAT TO WEAR

"What should I wear?" Most parents of teenage girls have heard that wail just before the next question, "Can you take me to the mall?" Luckily, most dogs don't want to go shopping, but they do need clothing (commonly called equipment) to help them act in a civilized manner.

Equipment can be quite confusing. There's the "goth" look, with pinch or spike collars and choke chains; there's the "conservative" look, with normal flat collars or harnesses; and there's also the "fashionable" look, complete with designer collars and leashes and even scarves and booties.

Sometimes people think choosing the right equipment will make their dog behave well. Sorry—it doesn't work that way! Equipment can be compared to pen and paper or a computer keyboard. You can't write without them, but they don't write on their own.

Before you actually choose some equipment, let's see how different gear works. Collars are the most important.

Collars

Choke Chain Collars

One of the most "popular" collars is a choke chain, often called a "training" collar. It works by choking the dog when he does something the handler doesn't like—such as pulling on the leash. As far as I'm concerned, there's very little about this collar to recommend it. It's not even pretty! Inexperienced handlers usually have a great deal of trouble using it properly, and their dogs continue to pull while gasping and choking. The choke chain can injure your dog if you're not careful, and you can actually harm his trachea through pulling or jerking. Another dog might injure him by catching a tooth in his collar during play, or your dog could harm himself by catching the collar on a fence and choking.

Flat collars are good articles on which to hang your dog's identification.

Some experienced trainers find the choke chain useful, but many of us who originally used it have long since moved to other collars.

Pinch/Spike/Prong Collars

A pinch, spike, or prong collar works by closing around the dog's neck as he starts to pull on the leash. When he reaches a certain point, the prongs pinch the skin and cause discomfort. This in turn causes the dog to slow down. Whether the action of the collar causes actual pain or not depends on your outlook. I think it does, especially given that many dogs yelp when the collar tightens. A dog's neck is not as delicate as a human's is, but it isn't made out of steel either (although when a dog is pulling you down the street, it can feel like it). Both the choke chain and pinch collar use pain and discomfort to punish the dog for pulling. To me, using this type of collar is reminiscent of the now obsolete classroom practice of striking children with a ruler to discourage bad behavior.

Martingale Collars

A martingale collar is designed like a pinch collar without the prongs, and therefore, without the pain. Another name for it is a "limited slip" collar. As a restraint device, it works well with dogs who aren't really interested in investigating the world when you want to walk, but it doesn't work well on dogs who really pull.

Regular (Flat) Collars

A regular (flat) collar is a nice article of clothing on which to hang your dog's identification, and it's useful to attach your leash to if your relationship is such that you and your dog walk together comfortably. However, it's not much use as a training device.

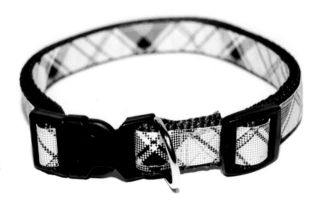

Head Collars

Another device is a head collar, which is really a halter like one that you would use on a horse. This collar gives you a lot of control over the dog's head, and when you control the head, you pretty much control the dog. There are positive and negative aspects to the halter. Although you have a lot more control with this type of device, you need substantial leash savvy to use it properly. Pull too hard and you'll twist the dog's head back. Pull up, and his head will go with it. The other disadvantages are twofold: Both owners and dogs don't like them much. The halter looks a bit like a muzzle, and passersby often shy away from a dog who is wearing one. (However, as they've become more popular, that reaction has lessened.) More importantly, many dogs object vehemently to wearing a head collar. They rub their muzzles on the ground and between

CASE STUDY

FINDING A COMMON LANGUAGE

One of the best things about training your dog is coming up with a common language. For some reason, many people think that dogs already know how to understand us, but of course they don't. Take Mary, who adopted an adolescent Border Collie mix, Foxy. Foxy was very bright, and Mary didn't think she needed to take training classes. Maybe Foxy didn't, but it seems Mary did. When Mary called, Foxy took it under advisement. When Mary cued Foxy to sit or down, Foxy seemed to think it was a suggestion rather than an instruction. Mary figured that Foxy was defiant and began to shout her commands, which just made Foxy afraid of her. Within a few weeks, Foxy actually ran away when she was called, or for that matter, asked to do anything. That made Mary even more frustrated, so she hired a dog trainer who told her she should use an electronic collar on Foxy if she ever wanted to get control. Luckily, Mary decided that that might not be the best idea. She came for a consult and a subsequent class, and the two have lived happily (well, mostly happily) ever since.

your legs and sometimes can't concentrate at all on what you'd like them to do. It's probably like owning a very badly fitted pair of glasses that you must wear. Some dogs get used to the head collar right away, some take time, and some never do acclimate to wearing it.

Harnesses

There are a number of harnesses on the market. Many have a nice, fashionable look, and some are actually very useful. I like them because they avoid the neck area and distribute pressure evenly most of the time. However, harnesses that have a leash attachment on the back often almost encourage pulling—just look at how sled dogs pull! There are a few no-pull harnesses available; most work by applying pressure to the back of the dog's front legs. Some work well, but many chafe under the legs.

The harness type I like best seems counterintuitive. The leash attachment is in the front, rather than on the dog's back. This controls the opposition reflex so that when the dog pulls, he actually does a U-turn. It's very humane and causes no pain, either to the dog or to you. I think it enhances the dog/guardian relationship. Although it's best if you get instructions on how to use this type of harness, it's virtually impossible to injure a dog with it.

Leashes

I have just two criteria for a leash: It must be comfortable to hold (soft and pliable), and it should not be a retractable leash. Many people do use retractable leashes, but they aren't suitable for training. Indeed, they can actually encourage pulling on

A nylon leash makes a good choice for small to medium dogs.

the leash, and they can be dangerous if they get tangled around your legs, your dog's legs, strangers' legs, or around trees. I use a short, 2- to 3-foot (0.5- to 1-m) leash for training a dog to walk next to me, a 6-foot (2-m) leash for most other work, and a long line (30 feet [9 m]) to teach a dog to come when called.

If you have a small dog, pretty much any material will do, as your dog is not likely to pull too hard. However, for medium to small dogs, I suggest leather or a soft nylon that won't dig into your hands. I don't recommend chain leashes except in cases where the dog is biting at or chewing through his normal leash. They're heavy and cumbersome, and they interfere with good communication. When you hold your leash, try not to put the loop around your wrist. If your dog does pull hard, it can injure your hand. Instead, make an "accordion" out of the excess leash, and hold it in your hand.

TRAINING STAGES

To make the training process as successful as possible, it helps if you understand some of the precepts of training before you begin. If you're consistent, your dog will improve very quickly. There are just two stages of training: acquisition and maintenance. Acquisition is the learning of a behavior, and maintenance is sustaining the learned behavior.

Acquisition

During acquisition, your dog begins the process of understanding what you want. If you use inducements to help him learn, he will learn faster. If you use punishment, he might perform the behavior, but he will become cautious around you and you may get what is called "behavioral fallout." Although your dog is doing what you want, the attitude may be depressed, or he may lash out at another dog or person.

During the acquisition stage, you should reward your dog every time he carries out the behavior. Just because you use a treat every time your dog performs the exercise, however, doesn't mean that he has to see the treat before the behavior. And that's where most people go wrong. The dog learns that he has to do something when a certain "picture" is in front of him. There you are—standing, treat in hand, saying "Sit." If the dog doesn't see the treat, the picture isn't complete and he won't execute the behavior. To be truly successful, then, you must switch from a visible treat to a hidden treat very quickly indeed, within 15 to 20 repetitions, if possible. Once you do that, the dog will begin to work for you without looking for the reward first.

This technique seems easy, so why don't people use it? There are a couple of reasons. Mostly, we're impatient. Dog sits, gets treat. Dog sits, gets treat. Owner hides treat, dog doesn't sit. Owner gets impatient, brings out treat, picture is complete: Dog sits, gets treat. Success! Owner whines "My dog will only do a *sit* when he sees a treat." The other reason has to do with guilt. Once we start giving treats, it's difficult for us to hide them or stop giving them. Try to get past the guilt, and your dog will start working for you instead of the food.

When you're teaching a complex exercise, split it into increments. The dog needs to be sure of what you want. Much of the time dogs just guess; sometimes they guess right and sometimes they guess wrong. (Think of trying to ask a Bulgarian who

Acquisition is the learning of a behavior.

doesn't speak English where the restroom is and you'll understand what I mean. You'll luck out eventually, but you won't know quite what words or gestures did it!) We often think that dogs know what we mean because they look so interested and alert, as though they understand everything we say. They don't.

If your dog now knows the behavior (he performs it perfectly with the treat hidden, and you are rewarding him each and every time he does it), where do we go from here? It is time to begin to vary the sequencing of behavior and rewards.

Variable Reinforcement

First, you'll start asking for two behaviors for the price of one. Ask for a *sit*. Release your dog with a release word. Quickly ask for another *sit*. Mark and treat—you just got two behaviors for one reward (more on this later). This is called variable or random reinforcement. You are asking for more behaviors per reward as your dog performs more reliably.

In addition to requesting two behaviors for one reward, you'll also begin adding other behaviors. Let's say your dog knows *sit* and *lie down* really well. If you say "Sit," he sits. If you say "Lie down," down he goes. Now combine them so that the

When you're teaching a complex exercise, split it into increments.

sequence is sit, lie down, (treat), sit, lie down, (treat). And every once in a while, try sit, (treat), lie down, (treat). You can go on "chaining" behaviors in any number of ways, following sequences such as sit, down, come, wait, roll over, (treat), but remember to make the sequence random: Sometimes treat after only one exercise, or your dog may learn to skip the first two behaviors because he knows the third one will be rewarded.

Maintenance

Even though your dog may have learned his lessons well, you still shouldn't stop training or rewarding him. This is where the maintenance stage comes in. Here's an example from our human world that explains why maintenance is so important. Imagine your teenage daughter is learning to use a computer. In the beginning, her instructor praises her when she starts a program and types a rudimentary sentence. As she improves, the congratulations come when she accomplishes

During the maintenance stage, it is important to reward your dog for success.

something more challenging. (That's what we're doing here with our dogs—raising the criteria.) Eventually, her skill on the computer lands her a job, which brings its own rewards—primarily money. She keeps getting better until she is very good and knows her computer inside out. One day her employer says "You're darn good at that computer stuff. You're so good that we're going to stop paying you!" I don't know about her, but I'd quit! There's only so much we humans want to do for praise alone. However, many people want to stop rewarding their dogs altogether. If you discontinue the rewards, the learned behaviors will start deteriorating over time and perhaps even disappear. Thus, it's crucial that you don't ever stop "paying" your dog; you just need to adjust the pay as the workload changes. As you will discover, it takes quite some time to get to the maintenance stage!

Chapter Eleven

Obedience Training

What is obedience training? Actually, in the dog training world, it's just a few little exercises that can help you and your dog get along for the next 14 years or so. However, these exercises won't teach your dog obedience in the sense that he will be waiting with bated breath for you to tell him what to do. Dogs—especially adolescent dogs—just don't do that, any more than kids do. They obey the rules because they have to obey the rules, not because the rules make sense to them. (It's good to continually remind yourself that what you want is not necessarily what they want. In fact, it's not likely to ever be what they want.)

We should be thoughtful and clear about what we demand of our furry friends. I know what I want—safety first! I want my dogs to "hold my hand" when we're walking and not to pull ahead. I want them to come when I call them and to refrain from ingesting cat waste or other unsavory things. These behaviors may not seem difficult, but because we're fighting our dogs' instincts, they can be hard for them to learn. But they can learn them, so let's get started.

VERBAL CUES

There are a couple of very important verbal signals you should know before you begin any training that requires some precision. These include the "marker word" and the "release word."

Marker Word, or "You Did That Right!"

The marker word or "bridge" lets you "mark" the instant your dog does something that you like. After marking a behavior, you deliver a reward. I suggest that you use the verbal "yes!" or try using a clicker, a device that emits a click when you press it.

The marker is not praise; it's just a snapshot of the behavior you want. You need the snapshot so that you and your dog are clear about the desired behavior. Often, it's quite difficult to actually reward the dog while the behavior is in progress, so marking it is a great way to bridge the behavior and the delivery of the treat.

1. To teach your dog what the marker means, relax with him in a comfortable spot without many distractions.
2. Make your marker sound ("yes" or use a clicker), and then give your dog a treat.
3. Repeat that sequence 20 or 30 times during the session. Repeat the session at least two or three times over the next day or so.

4. Your dog will learn to associate the marker sound with the delivery of a treat. You'll know that you've been successful if you make the sound at some random moment and your dog immediately looks at you or comes running to get a treat.

There is another kind of marker word. It's called the NRM or "no reward mark," and it's given when the dog doesn't do what he is asked. There are a variety of words to use: "uh uh," "try again," "too bad," or "wrong" are examples. Refrain from using any of these words until your dog has an idea of what he should be doing. That means that you'll need a lot of successful performances before you use the NRM.

A marker word allows you to "mark" the instant your dog does something that you like.

Release Word, or "You Can Go Do What You Want Now"

The other word you should pick is your "release word." The release word tells your dog that he no longer has to hold the position you put him in, whether it's *sit*, *down*, or *heel*. This word is the cue that makes you the boss because your dog isn't supposed to release himself. It's the bell that lets the kids out of the classroom or says "You're excused." Once you have chosen the release word, it should stay consistent throughout your dog's life.

I suggest that you choose a word that you don't use on a daily basis. "Release" is a very good one. Others are "dismissed," "go play," "at ease," "that'll do," or even "you're excused!" "Okay" is problematic because we speak that word in conversation all the time. At any rate, when you release your dog, you should say his name first to get his attention and to differentiate the selection of that word from the other times you use it. It's also a good idea to use a particular inflection with your release word, as in "RE-lease" or "DIS-missed." "Good dog" is usually praise (and faint praise at that) and generally not a good release word. An interesting choice is to say your dog's name in a singsong voice—it sounds very different to the dog, and it's easy to remember.

Use the release word to release your dog from an exercise. When you've decided that the exercise is at an end, say the release word you have chosen, then step away from your dog. You might even clap your hands or give him a tiny little bow.

To teach your dog what the release word means:

1. Ask him to do something he most likely already knows how to do, such as sit.
2. When he's sitting, give him a little treat, then say your release word and let him get up.
3. Repeat about five times and he'll begin to understand what you mean.

WATCH ME, OR "PAY ATTENTION WHEN I'M TALKING TO YOU!"

Talking to your kid when she is not looking at you is one of the more frustrating aspects of being a parent. You feel like you're not getting through to her (and you're usually right). Getting eye contact from your dog is important.[1] In fact, holding that eye contact for a few seconds is just as important. This section outlines a few ways to teach this lesson.

Method 1: Use a Leash

One method that works very well is to put your dog on a leash and either step on it or attach it to something immovable. This is so that you don't have to hold the leash, but your dog has to stay in the general vicinity.

1. Hold a treat behind you and say your dog's name.
2. If he looks at you, mark and treat. If he doesn't look at you, just wait. You can move around a bit to remind him that you're there, but try not to talk. Because he can't go anywhere interesting, he's bound to look at you sooner or later.
3. When your dog looks at you, mark and treat.
4. Now say his name again, wait for him to look at you, and mark and treat. Do this

---

[1] Shy or sensitive dogs often don't like to make eye contact, which they see as threatening. I suggest just having those dogs look at your face.

again and again. Try very hard not to say his name over and over again, as then he will just learn that you nag.

5. After he gets pretty good at looking at you, wait until he actually looks into your eyes before you mark and treat.

It's important to raise the criteria as learning progresses. You would praise your first grader for spelling her name correctly, but you wouldn't continue to do so when she was in high school, right? You'd praise better and better spelling as she advanced in the learning process. Eventually, you'd like your child to spell something like "anti-disestablishmentarianism." Then you'd really lavish praise on her, especially because her ability would put her in a tiny minority of spellers. At any rate, as you work with your dog on his eye contact, praise for faster looks—what we call

With most dogs, getting eye contact is extremely important.

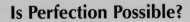

Is Perfection Possible?

Perfection is not possible. One hundred percent recalls are not possible. One hundred percent sits are not possible. Even those people who brag that their dogs are totally reliable are wrong. If you want something that's 100 percent reliable, get a pet rock. Your dog will not be perfect until you are. If you think you may be expecting too much from your dog, ask yourself the following questions:

❖ Is my dog capable of doing the behavior physically?
❖ Have I trained the behavior until my dog is 90 percent reliable?
❖ Have I trained my dog in this environment before?

If you answered yes to all of these questions, then you are not asking too much. If you answered no, then you should go back to work proofing the behaviors.

a good head snap. Try practicing this method when your dog is in front of you or trotting away from you. If you say his name and he immediately turns and looks at you, this could be the time for a "jackpot" (several treats delivered one at a time, accompanied by immense praise).

Method 2: Use Props

If you don't have enough patience for this first method, you can use some props. You might do this in private, as some may think that it looks rather silly.

1. Hold a treat in your hand.
2. Say your dog's name and sweep your hand from his nose up to your forehead.
3. As soon as he looks at the treat, mark the behavior and pop the treat into his mouth. If he has a favorite toy, you can use that on your forehead instead of the treat.
4. Repeat again and again, and then begin raising your criteria. Wait until he looks into your eyes as opposed to just looking at the treat before you mark the behavior.
5. Now put the motivator (treat, ball, or toy) behind your back and call your dog's name.
6. When you get eye contact, mark and treat.
7. Repeat the exercise several times.

8. Next, hold the motivator at arm's length. Your dog must look at you, not the motivator, to receive the reward. (This is very Zen. In order to get the treat, he must look away from the treat.) Pretty soon you'll have a dog who looks you straight in the eye whenever you call his name.
9. To prove this, call his name when he is otherwise engaged—if he turns and looks at you, mark and jackpot.

Add Another Cue

Once your dog is responding when he hears his name, you can add another cue, like *watch* or *look*. To accomplish this:

1. Say your dog's name, followed by the word "watch," and then mark and treat.
2. Repeat several times and then begin to wait a second or so after your cue before you mark and treat. What you're doing is delaying the marker so that he'll look at you longer.
3. Work up to three to five seconds of attention. That's actually a lot longer than you think.
4. While he's looking at you, praise him verbally. ("Wonderful, excellent, good job!") This will help him sustain the eye contact.

By the way, I don't think that your dog always has to watch you, but he should always know where you are. Hide-and-seek (you hide, he seeks) is a great game that will teach him to pay attention to your unpredictability. I especially like hiding on walks in the woods when my dogs are several yards (m) ahead of me. I hide behind a tree, then call their names and get very excited when they find me. People might think I'm a tad on the crazy side, but I don't care. As a result of this game, my dogs are always keeping an eye on me.

Now that you have your dog's attention and he knows that you have what he wants (treats, balls, or toys), you can teach him what you want him to do.

SIT: THE EASIEST EXERCISE

Let's face it—your dog already knows how to sit. This exercise is aimed at having him sit when you want him to and not just when he wants to. Working on *sit* is also a great way to teach him that lessons have now commenced and it's time to pay attention.

Method 1: Lure the Behavior

My preferred method for teaching *sit* is to use a lure in the form of a treat in your hand.

1. Attach the leash to your dog and either step on it or let it drag.
2. Get his attention by saying his name, and when he looks at you, give him a little bit of the treat. Then use the rest of it to lure him into the *sit* position.
3. Slowly move your hand just over his head. As he leans back to follow the treat, he'll probably sit. (Don't hold the treat too high; otherwise, he may jump up to get it—not what you want!) Try not to touch him with your hands. If he sits voluntarily, he'll remember it better.
4. When he sits, mark and treat. He'll get up almost immediately, which is okay to begin with.

A game of hide-and-seek, in which you hide and your dog seeks, will teach him to pay attention to your unpredictability.

5. Lure the behavior at least three or four times.
6. When he's successfully following your hand and dropping into a *sit*, say "Sit" as you move your hand over his head without the treat in it.
7. If he sits, mark and treat. If he doesn't, wait a bit and then repeat the exercise. If he still doesn't give you a *sit*, go back to the lure with the treat, practice that a few times, and then remove the treat. Don't continue until he'll sit without a treat in your hand. However, do remember to mark and treat. The treat should just come from the other hand.
8. When he starts to sit for longer than a nanosecond, delay your marker. The sequence should go more or less like this the first

few times: "Patches, sit! Yes!" (treat). Once he has the idea, you can delay the mark and treat to extend the *sit* a bit: "Patches, sit." (beat) "Yes!" (mark and treat). After that, you can add the release word so the progression will go like this: "Patches, sit!" (couple of seconds) "Yes!" (treat). "Release!"

Method 2: Capture the Behavior

It's also possible to teach *sit* by simply waiting for the behavior to occur. This technique is called "capturing" a behavior. If your dog sits without prompting, you can mark and reward.

Method 3: Model the Behavior

You can also very gently push on your dog's rump to show him what you want. However, many dogs forget what they're doing and turn to look at you when you do that, so it sometimes backfires. Dogs, like people, learn much more rapidly without physical pressure. In fact, when pressure is applied, dogs and people tend to push back. (This is called the "opposition reflex.") Children know this instinctively and often demand that their parents let them "do it by themselves." Learning any skill is much easier if you are led or prompted—anything but manhandled.

LIE DOWN

Here is another exercise that your dog already knows. However, just because he knows how to lie down doesn't mean that it's easy to perform on cue. Many dogs resist being told to lie down. It's probably sort of humiliating and intimidating because the position allows people to tower over them.

Method 1: Lure the Behavior

Again, the lure is the preferred method. Your dog can be in a sitting or standing position; I prefer to teach *lie down* from a *stand*, but it's not particularly important at this stage.

1. Give your dog a small treat.
2. Now, showing him that you have another treat, move your lure hand quickly down in front of him and then draw it forward.
3. If all goes well, he should lie down. As he does so, say "Lie down."
4. Mark and treat when his whole body is on the floor.

With patience and persistence, you can teach your dog to lie down on command.

Sometimes all doesn't go well and your dog won't drop down. Alternative methods include holding the treat between his two front paws so that he has to buckle and drop to get it or moving it close to his side on the floor. As he reaches around to get it, he will curl into a "C" and drop into the *down*. When he hits the ground, mark and treat.

As with the *sit*, after several repetitions, put the treat in your other hand and lure without the treat. If you are successful, mark and deliver your treat out of your other hand. One of the complaints I hear from my clients is "My dog is only obedient when I show him the treat first." This method eliminates that problem and also sets you up for intermittent or random reinforcement.

Sometimes dogs refuse to be lured the easy way. If you're willing to experiment, you can try a few other methods: You can sit on the floor with one knee up and lure the dog under that knee; you can lure him under a chair or low table; or you can just wait him out. Step on his leash so that he won't wander off, show him the lure, hold it on the ground, and wait. Eventually, most dogs will drop into a *down*, at which point you should mark and reward.

Method 2: Model the Behavior

If luring fails, you can try modeling, which is physically helping your dog into position. (This is help, not force.)

1. Kneel down beside the dog on his right side, and place your left hand on his shoulders. Use your right hand to lure him with the treat.

2. If that doesn't work, try putting your right hand behind his front legs while gently putting pressure on his shoulder blades with your left hand. As mentioned before, the lure is much more effective than physically manipulating your dog; you're likely to encounter a lot more resistance with this method.

3. If your dog growls when you try placing him into the *down*, immediately stop the training session and take a time-out. You'll need to reexamine your relationship with your dog and make sure that he sees you as a leader. He must regard you as such before he'll allow you to make him lie down on command.

4. In any case, when he's prone, mark and reward. Most dogs will pop up immediately, which is fine.

5. Continue with more repetitions, and as he gets better, delay the mark until he's been down for a few seconds. You can give him a couple more treats while he's lying down, and tell him what a wonderful dog he is. When you're ready, mark and treat, and follow with your release word.

Don't get angry, even if you think that your dog is very stubborn and he behaves as though he will never lie down. He's probably confused, and when he understands, he'll comply—if you're patient. It takes some dogs a long time.

STAY

Both *sit* and *lie down* are much more valuable if the dog actually stays in the position for more than an instant. As a result, we need to add the *stay*. The word "stay" causes conflict in the dog-training world. Some trainers maintain that you shouldn't have to say "Stay" because the dog is supposed to remain sitting or lying down until he's released. It's probably true, but the word "stay" adds clarity, and there isn't anything wrong with that.

When your dog has a solid *stay*, you can start to work on distance.

Method: Lure the Behavior

At any rate, to add the *stay* to the *sit* exercise:

1. Cue your dog to sit.
2. Next say "Stay" while holding the palm of your hand in front of his face for a second or so.
3. Put your hand away and hold a few treats about 2 feet (0.5 m) away from him. Give him one, then another, and then release him. He's being rewarded for staying in position—an easy task. It's as though you asked your child to sit in a chair and then every few seconds gave her a ten-dollar bill. Chances are she would sit in that chair for a very long time.
4. Now we will make the exercise a bit harder. Begin to lower your hand with the lure in it a couple of feet (m) away from the dog's head.
5. If he gets up, use your NRM (the no reward marker that you've chosen), close your fist around the treat, and raise your hand to its original position. Begin again.
6. When you can lower the lure to the ground (while holding it), mark the behavior and pop the treat into his mouth. Make sure that he's still sitting when the treat goes into his mouth.
7. After he's taken it, release him.
8. Repeat, remembering to deliver the reinforcement (treat) when he is in the position you have asked for.[2]
9. Now, while he is sitting, put several treats on the ground. Pick one up and give it to him while praising him. Repeat your *stay* cue and then pick up the next treat.

[2] This is a very important concept. The reinforcement (treat) should be delivered where you want the dog to go. If you give the dog a treat at chest level, he will learn to jump for it. If you want him to lie down and you give him the treat on or close to the ground, he'll tend to stay there. If you want him to sit, treat him at the level of his head.

Lying Down on Cue

If your dog is already a good retriever, you can play a game that includes lying down on cue. Use the ball as a lure. When your dog drops to the ground, mark and then quickly throw the ball behind him. Retrieving the ball is his reward. After he's given the ball back to you, repeat the process. With enough repetitions, you will have a fast and reliable *down*.

10. After you've picked up the last treat, release him from the exercise. After many repetitions, he should have the concept. Then you can slowly stop using the treats.

When you teach *sit* and *down*, you'll use your marker word to mark the right behavior. However, when you teach *stay*, you don't need to use it. Instead, use the release word. This is because there is no "snapshot" of the behavior as there is with *sit* and *down*.

Duration

After you and your dog have grasped the idea, you can work on duration (time in the position) and then distance.

1. First, extend the time of the *stay* until he can stay for two minutes or so.
2. When he's successfully maintaining the *stay* 90 percent of the time, ask a family member or friend to do things that would ordinarily distract him while he's in a *stay*, like petting him, throwing a ball around him, or anything your dog might find entrancing.
3. Remain close to your dog while he's being distracted so that you'll be able to reinforce the *stay* or put him back in the proper position should he get up. If your dog is easily distracted, stay right next to him.
4. Whenever a distraction goes by, such as a ball bouncing or person walking, give him a treat at the same time and tell him how good he is. This is especially helpful for nervous or high-strung dogs.

Distance

When your dog has a pretty solid *stay*, you can start to work on distance. Most people want to work on distance first, but that's usually a bad idea. If he decides to get up and leave when you're 8 feet (2.5 m) away, what are you going to do? If you catch him, you'll have to start all over. It's much better to "proof" the exercise when you're close by, as we just discussed.

1. Ask your dog to stay and then move a couple of feet (m) away.
2. Return to him fairly quickly, and reinforce while he is still in position.
3. Cue him to stay again and walk away while keeping a close eye on him.
4. Reinforce at intervals during the entire *stay* so that he wants to remain in position.
5. When you're ready to release him from the *stay*, return to him and do so. I recommend that you always return to your dog before releasing him; it's a good way to teach him to wait to be released.

Stay From Lie Down

Apply the same progression when you teach him to stay lying down. Dogs can easily hold a *sit-stay* for about a minute. If you'd like your dog to stay longer, you should cue him to lie down, as that's more comfortable. I recommend that you aim for a one-minute *sit-stay* and a three-minute *down-stay*. Eventually, he should be able to remain lying down in the *stay* for 15 to 20 minutes—or even longer.

WAIT FOR ME

The *wait* teaches your dog to stop when you cue him to and to wait to be released. The major difference between *wait* and *stay* is that *stay* requires a dog to freeze in a particular position. The dog doesn't have to freeze when you tell him to wait. He just has to stop where he is, as though a wall just dropped down in front of him. For example, if you tell your dog to wait at the front door while you exit, he can move about in the room, but he cannot go through the door.

This is a pretty handy little exercise. In fact, it's the one I use the most. My dogs have to wait before exiting the car and going out the door. Occasionally, I ask them to wait when they're too far ahead of me. *Wait* is easy to teach and uses your body as well as your voice.

Method: The Threshold Method

The easiest way to teach your dog to wait is to use a door or threshold as a boundary over which the dog shouldn't pass.

1. Back through the threshold with the dog in front of you.
2. As you go through, cue your dog to wait. Rock slightly forward toward him to help him stop.
3. When he has stopped, you can start to back out again.
4. If he follows you, tell him "wait" again and gently push him back with your body if necessary.
5. When you can back out and he doesn't follow you, turn slightly to the side and release him. ("Okay.")
6. Once he has mastered that, you can walk through the door with him and cue him to wait using your hand (fingers down, palm facing the dog). Be prepared to body block him if he doesn't listen.
7. When your dog is on one side and you are on the other, count to five slowly to yourself. Then release him through the door. Many dogs will offer a *sit* while they're waiting. That's perfectly fine but not necessarily a part of the exercise.

You can use the *wait* command before going out the door.

Some doors, such as car doors, front doors, and perhaps the back door, should be designated "permanent" wait doors. This means that your dog never goes through them at any time unless someone is there to give him permission. To establish a permanent *wait* at doorways:

1. First make sure that your dog understands the *wait*.

2. Then, without giving the command, open the door and start to step through.
3. If your dog starts to go with you, use your NRM and block the door.
4. Repeat until he understands that he has to wait at this particular door even though no command has been given.
5. When it's obvious he understands the concept, step through the door, wait a few seconds, and then release him.

LEAVE IT—DON'T TOUCH THAT ICKY THING!

This is a nice exercise that comes in very handy if you drop a steak or pass a dead skunk. It tells your dog that whatever he's looking at is definitely not his. We teach it by not letting him get to the attraction!

Method: Swap for a Treat
1. First, step on your leash or let it drag.
2. Offer a treat to your dog, and as he reaches for it, cue him to "take it."
3. Now hold a treat in each hand, keeping one hand behind your back. Open the other hand, and when your dog reaches for the treat, say "Leave it" and close your hand over the treat.
4. Do this again and again and again. Patience is the key here—it sometimes takes 20 times before the dog stops pawing or nudging for the treat and looking at you in confusion.
5. When he backs away and looks at you questioningly (*Why are you showing me the food if you don't intend to give it to me?*), praise him, close that hand, and offer him the treat in the other hand, saying "Take it." Don't give him the *leave it* treat or he may just stare at your hand until it opens up.
6. Next, tie your dog's leash to something immovable and show him that you have a treat.
7. Slowly put the treat down beside you and say "Leave it."
8. When your dog goes for it, step in his way and say "Leave it" at the same time. If he's like most dogs, he'll try to go around you. You—being very coordinated—will keep your body between him and the food. If you need to, step on the treat to avoid having him get it. Within seconds, most dogs get discouraged, back up, and sit.
9. When he looks at you, mark and give him a treat from your hand. Don't let him get the other one. Pretend it's a dead skunk or some moldy old hamburger—surely you wouldn't want him to have those things, would you?

TOUCH OR TARGET

If you want your dog to follow your hand cues, you can teach him to follow your hand and touch it. This technique also reduces the use of the treat quickly. The purpose of this exercise is to teach your dog to watch your hand for instructions.

Method: Follow Your Hand

1. Begin by showing your dog your fist or two fingers extended from your fist just a few inches (cm) from his nose. He'll probably investigate your fist curiously.
2. When he touches it with his nose, mark and reward him with a treat from the other hand.
3. Repeat five times, then rest for ten seconds and do it again. Try not to follow his nose with your fist; this doesn't teach him much except that you'll follow him. Some dogs will touch your hand the first few times and then lose interest. If you wait and try again in a few minutes, he's likely to touch your fist again. If he's totally lost

The *leave it* command tells your dog that he's not to touch whatever he's eyeing.

interest, you can put your other hand—with a treat in it—right behind the target fist a few times to perk him up. Then go back to the previous method. It's really best if your dog doesn't see or smell the treat until he hears the marker word.

4. When he is touching your hand consistently, add the cue. ("Touch," "target," or "here" are common.) Give the cue just as he's about to touch your fist. If you think that he's grasped the concept, move your fist slightly and see if he follows to touch it. He should stretch out his neck to touch your fist.

5. Practice your verbal cue many times. When he's pretty reliable, stop giving him a treat when he touches your palm with no verbal signal, and only reinforce when you've cued him.

6. Move your hand to a variety of places, making him work to touch it. Be very careful not to extend the behavior too quickly, as the dog could get discouraged. The hardest place for him to follow your hand is up, so keep your "target" low for the first several sessions.

Basic obedience training is a must for every dog.

Once he fully understands how to target your fist, you can begin to use it for a variety of behaviors, including loose leash walking. As you walk, hold your hand to your side and ask him to touch it. Mark and reward each time, and then gradually extend the time between "touches." I've also found targeting to be an excellent way to move resting dogs. (They can become very heavy if you try to shift them physically.) Just signal a touch and they will get up and move themselves. Targeting is also used extensively in trick training. In fact, it would be very difficult to teach dogs tricks without it.

RECALL (COME)

Here's the exercise you've been waiting for—and it's one of the hardest to teach! Before we begin, here are some very important rules about the *recall*:

❖ Never say "Come" if you really don't think that your dog is going to come to you. Use another word ("here" or "hurry up") or go get him. If you've been using the word "come" unsuccessfully for a while, it might be wise to change his recall word so that he doesn't have the wrong association with it.

❖ Never punish him if he didn't come the first time you called. You, not your dog, blew it! Give in gracefully and practice some more.

❖ Never call your dog to you to punish him. (For example, if he chewed up your shoe and you want to tell him about it, don't call him to you and scold him. You'll only teach him that coming when called gets him in trouble.)

Now on to the exercise. I've broken it down into several parts because it's actually a complicated move requiring your dog to make a series of decisions. Let's say he's facing away from you when you call. First, he must stop what he's doing; second, he must turn and look at you; and third, he must come running to you.

Part 1: Reward For Collar Hold

Many dogs, especially adolescents, are adept at running to you, only to do a fly-by: racing past you or dancing just out of your reach. You can prevent this problem by teaching your dog that the reward comes when you have hold of his collar:

1. Begin by having your dog sit next to you.
2. Say "Gotcha" as you are reaching for his collar. Quickly pop a treat into his mouth. Thus, the sequence should go: "Gotcha" (grab collar) (treat).
3. Practice this five or six times a day. Start gently and work up to a pretty strong grab.

Part 2: Employ the Slack Leash

1. With your dog on a slack leash and a treat in one hand, walk forward a few steps.
2. As you're walking, suddenly stop and move backward, going into reverse. As you do, call your dog in an excruciatingly happy voice, "PUPPY, COOOMMME!"
3. Take two or three steps backward and then stop, holding your treat at waist level. Your dog should come to you automatically and sit in front of you.
   Mark his behavior when he starts toward you. Slip your hand under his collar, smile, and reward him.

Part 3: Strengthen Your Recall

Here are a couple of steps to strengthen the *recall* before you really put it to the test.

1. Use a treat to guide your dog into a *sit* by holding it in front of you, then raising it slightly upward until it's at your waistline. Your dog should just glide into a *sit*.
2. If he's coming fairly slowly, move backward while calling him in an excited tone.

With several repetitions, your dog should begin to understand the word "come." However, this doesn't mean that he knows he's supposed to come to you whenever and wherever he hears that word. You'll have to teach him to "generalize" this behavior.

All About Place Learning

Before we get into that, we need to discuss a phenomenon called "place learning." Often kids will be well behaved in school, but when they get home it's a different matter. Maybe your pleasant, cooperative teenager becomes a sullen, uncooperative teenager at home. Or maybe she is quiet and reserved at school or at a dance and a wild extrovert at home. Where she is has a great deal to do with what she does and how she acts. Adults can be like this too. Our behavior at work may be radically different from what it is at home.

It shouldn't come as a surprise that dogs are exactly the same. Perhaps you've been teaching *lie down* in your backyard. When you proudly try to show off the behavior at a friend's house, you get a blank look as though he's never heard the word before. It's very embarrassing, as you insist that he "knows" it and is just being stubborn. If you think logically, you'll realize that he probably isn't being stubborn. Stubborn won't get him a treat, it won't get him praise, and it won't get him freedom. He's just confused because he didn't realize he was expected to do the same thing somewhere other than in your backyard. This is such a common phenomenon that for years I've visualized a T-shirt that says "He always does it at home" on one side and "He only does it here" on the other. We trainers hear both of these statements in our classes all the time.

Lack of generalization is particularly evident in the *recall*. A dog who races out of the yard into the house when you barely whisper for him to come develops total deafness when he's playing in a dog park or running on a trail. What this shows you, of course, is that you have to practice in a wide variety of locales before you can begin to get a reliable *recall*.

Practicing the *Recall*

Here are some fun ways to practice the *recall*:

Hide-and-Seek: You can do this in the house or outside. When your dog isn't paying attention to you, hide behind something (a door or a tree) and call him. You'll probably have to call him twice: once to get his attention, the second time to help him become oriented to your location. When he finds you, lavish praise on him and either give him some treats or play tug or another game he likes a lot. Dogs love this just as much as little kids do; sometimes just the act of finding is reward enough.

Find It: This is extraordinarily easy to teach, and dogs love it. It works on attention and the *recall* at the same time. First, let your dog see you put a treat on the ground. Then look at it, point to it, and say "Find it!" As your dog finds it, you

The *recall* teaches your dog to come to you on command.

should say "Yes," after which he'll probably look up to you for another treat. Repeat several more times, using your body and hand to guide your dog in the proper direction. After a few minutes of playing find it, begin to throw the treats on the ground farther and farther away. When you toss the treats, try to throw them across your dog's line of sight. If you throw them over his head, he won't be able to see them. Dogs see movement very well, and their peripheral vision is excellent, but they cannot distinguish something above their heads very well.

Next, toss the treat, and as he picks it up, say his name and tell him to come. ("Doggy, come!") He'll be motivated to come because he is continuing the game. If he doesn't come very fast, give him a treat when he gets to you, as well as the one that you've dropped on the ground. (Yes, you're being very generous here—aren't you a wonderful parent?) Finally, throw the treat as far away as you think he can go for it, and as he leaves, go in the opposite direction. Call him after he's picked up the treat, and reward him when he gets to you.

Round Robin: If there are several people in your household, practice *come* in a circle, calling your dog from person to person to be petted and rewarded. As he gets better, make your circle bigger. Then play the game with people placed in several locales in the house and then outside. Remember to praise your dog profusely when he gets to you.

Long-Line *Recall*: Take your dog to a place he's never been before, and make a big deal out of taking off his leash. Meanwhile, you've attached a light, 30-foot (9-m) long line to his harness or collar, and you're holding it gently so that there's no pressure on the leash. As he trots away from you, say his name and "Come!" If he turns around and comes to you, act very enthusiastic. If he doesn't come, give a quick, gentle tug on the line and start moving backward, urging him toward you. Reward him when he gets to you. Practice this a lot, gradually letting him get farther and farther away from you.

WALKING ON LEASH

Walking politely on leash is the most difficult exercise to teach, and we dog trainers have come up with several techniques for teaching it. I often use a combination, just to keep my dog focused on me. Before beginning, you must think about what a leash means to an untutored dog: It's a rope tied to his collar, allowing him to pull his owner wherever he, the dog, wants to go. We, of course, would like our dog to

Pulling behavior can be resolved by teaching your dog to walk nicely on leash.

see the leash as a rope that allows us to keep him by our side. Unfortunately, that takes some doing, so I've included a few methods to try. At least one should suit your training style and your dog's learning style.

With any method, you must remember that your dog needs to keep his attention on you. You cannot force this—it must come because you are being unpredictable while simultaneously being very rewarding. I call this being predictably unpredictable because your dog knows that you are likely to change direction or even disappear without much notice, and it's his job to make sure that he keeps track of you. The following are some methods you can try.

Method 1: Attention Walking

This is a good starting method for helping your dog see you as the center of the universe!

1. Begin with your dog sitting directly in front of you, facing you. Hold your leash very loosely, or tie it to your waist. Hold some soft, delicious treats in your hand.
2. Take a step or two backward and stop. Ask your dog to sit, then mark and treat.
3. Do this several times, making sure that you don't bump into something as you walk backward.
4. Now begin to extend the behavior, walking back for several feet (m) before you stop and reward.
5. After he's doing this easily (it takes maybe four minutes), begin walking backward and then abruptly walk into your dog, pushing him gently to your side. Take three or four steps, stop, and have him sit beside you rather than in front. Mark and treat.
6. Extend the behavior, each time making him go farther and farther beside you. If he begins to forge ahead, quickly step backward until he follows, then move into him again, making him walk beside you. Walk several steps, then stop, cue the *sit*, and mark and treat.
7. Later, as the behavior becomes reliable, add the verbal cue. As you begin walking, say "Walk with me" or "Let's go," pairing the cue with what he's doing right.

With any method of leash training, remember that your dog needs to keep his attention on you.

Method 2: Knotted Leash

This method gives you a physical reminder of how much leash you've decided to let your dog use. It's my favorite interim method.

1. Pick a word that tells your dog you're going to leave: "hey," "bye," "oops," "run," "yuck," or "oh oh." My favorite is "oops." I don't like using "no" because this word has a variety of emotions already attached to it.
2. Use a 6- or 8-foot (2- or 2.5-m) leash. Knot the leash about 18

inches to 2 feet (0.5 m) from the clasp. Assuming that your dog is on your left (the side most people prefer), hold the knot with your left hand. With your right hand, hold the loop at the end of the leash. He should be able to walk beside you and about 1 foot (0.5 m) behind or ahead of you without pulling the leash.

3. When you practice this method, walk your dog in a safe place where there are no other dogs. As you walk, watch his head and other body language very carefully. As soon as you lose his attention—he starts walking a little ahead of you, or to the side, or even looks away—give your good-bye signal and let the knot go. Hold on to the looped end of the leash with your right hand, and change direction. Your dog should catch up to you, and when he does, reinforce heavily with lots of praise and maybe a jackpot of treats.

4. Practice this method many times. For the knotted leash technique to be effective, it must be as automatic as putting your foot on the brake of your car.

Method 3: The Unreliable Leash

This method works well on dogs who are emotionally attached to their parents and who become nervous when left. Make sure that you're in a secure, enclosed location, as you're going to be letting go of your leash.

1. Hold the leash very lightly, giving your dog plenty of slack. As he draws ahead of you, say "Oops," let the leash slip all the way out of your hand, stop, and begin walking away.

2. When he notices you've gone and comes back to you, reinforce him (pets, praise, and treats) and begin walking forward again. Before long, he'll stop relying on the leash to let him know where you are.

Method 4: Target Walking

It's great to practice this method when you're on your way to the car, to a dog park, or anywhere else your dog really wants to go.

1. Place a delicious target (perhaps a bowl of cooked chicken!) about 20 feet (6 m) away from you. Make sure that your dog knows it's there. Now begin walking with your dog toward the target.

2. As soon as he steps ahead of you, say "Oops," stop, and walk back to your starting position, taking your dog along with you. Begin again. This may take many repetitions. When you finally reach the target without any pulling from your dog,

have him sit and give him the treats. You're teaching him that pulling doesn't get him where he wants to go.

Method 5: Find It

1. This method is fun for both you and your dog. At its most useful, find it distracts your dog from another dog or human. (It's handy when we trainers are working with aggression.) Begin by using the method I described for the *recall*.

2. Put a treat on the ground, point to it, and say "Find it!" After a few minutes of practice, begin to toss the treats on the ground, making sure to toss them across his line of sight. You'll notice that after your dog finds the treat, he always comes back to you for more. Now begin walking, and toss a treat gently on the floor in front of you. Say "Find it."

3. As your dog locates the treat, begin walking away, keeping your leash very loose or dropping it altogether. He'll get the treat and hurry to catch up to you. As he does, give him a cue to walk with you ("Let's go," "Walk with me," or whatever you want to use). Do this again and again. Drop the treat, say "Find it," and as soon as your dog finds it, move in a different direction. He is either looking for the treat or looking for you.

4. Begin to extend the behavior by walking farther and farther away between find its. If your dog is a confirmed puller, you can drop the treats just behind you and slightly to the left. He'll find them and hurry to catch up to you, but he's being reinforced for being behind you.

Method 6: The Double Leash

I usually try this method with a young puppy, but you can use it with an older dog as long as you apply it consistently. There are three essential ingredients: lots of soft, breakable treats, a regular 6-foot (2-m) leash, and a long line (a 20- to 30-foot [6- to 9-m] leash that can drag on the ground). The line should be light, but it doesn't have to be an "official" long line, which you can buy if you wish. However, nylon cording with knots every 3 feet (1 m) or so works just fine.

1. Begin by teaching your dog that being close to you is always rewarding. When he comes to you voluntarily, he should receive praise, petting, attention, and a treat or two. You might drop several small treats on the ground to make the area around you even more attractive. However, try not to be predictable about where the treats come

CASE STUDY

JEKYLL AND HYDE

One of my recent clients brought in her dog, Zeus, for a consult because he was beginning to behave aggressively toward other dogs when he was on leash. He'd lunge and bark and generally do a "Jekyll and Hyde" imitation: good dog one second, devil the next. When he did that, he wouldn't obey her at all—wouldn't sit, down, come, wait, or stop barking. Besides being mystified as to why he was doing this, she was furious with him. You see, he had aced the highest levels of obedience work in the ring. He was under perfect control, doing each and every exercise with precision and style.

What she didn't understand was place learning. As soon as Zeus left the ring, he in effect changed his clothes and took on a different persona. He certainly didn't understand that he was supposed to obey outside! We had to teach him that, as well as help the owner understand why he was lunging and what to do about it.

from; sometimes they will come from your hand (when he sits), and sometimes they will come from the ground.

2. Now attach the long line to your dog's collar—leave his regular leash off for right now. Let him drag the long line for a while until he begins to disregard it. This usually takes a few minutes.

3. As you begin to walk, he'll probably go ahead of you. When he gets to a point beyond which you do not want him to go, gently say "Wait" or "Stop" or "Close" (but pick one and use it consistently) to indicate that he's reached his limit. Immediately after you've said the word, step on the trailing leash. He'll come to an abrupt halt. Say his name and begin walking in another direction but not necessarily back the way you came. As soon as he catches up and begins walking by your side, praise and reward him with some delicious treats. Continue the walk. When he goes too far ahead, cue him to stop and step on the leash. When he comes back to you, praise, reward, and begin walking again. Repeat this exercise many, many times.

4. Once your dog is keeping an eye on you all the time, add his regular leash. Hold it very lightly and quite loosely. It should be loose enough to slip through your hand if

your dog pulls and you don't step on the trailing leash. Continue the same exercise, using your *stop* cue and without pulling on the regular leash at all. That leash should be there for looks and the law only, not for correcting. This is very important because dogs easily learn that pulling the leash forces you to go with them. I don't want my dog to learn that.

5. Go through the steps as before. (By now, the word "stop" or "wait" should be enough to stop your dog.) As you turn and walk in the other direction, if he walks by you, cue him with the words "walk with me" (or if you wish, "heel"). Twist, turn, and go in many different directions, often stopping and rewarding. Always keep your hands so loosely on the leash that he gets no cues from the leash—only from watching your body.

The easiest way to maintain good behavior is to work it into your lifestyle.

No matter which method you use, try to remember that you are the leader and your dog is the follower.

SUSTAINING GOOD BEHAVIOR

Often, when I'm consulting, clients will mention that they took their dog to class, but the dog doesn't seem to remember what was taught. One of my clients complained that her dog seemed to regard her commands as suggestions! Indeed, that sort of thing happens all the time, mostly because obedience lessons work against the dog's natural instincts and desires. Thus, if you would like your dog to continue to be civilized, you'll need to practice on a regular basis for the rest of the dog's life. This, as I noted earlier, is maintenance.

CHECKLIST

❖ The most important words for us to remember when training are the marker and release words. The first tells the dog he's doing something right, the second that the exercise is over.

❖ Remember to break down complicated exercises, teaching bit by bit so that it's easier for your dog to remember them.

❖ Vary where you practice if you want your dog to obey you in different places.

❖ Don't give your dog too much responsibility too soon—many people have lost their dog because they thought the *recall* had been perfected.

The easiest way to maintain good behavior is to work it into your lifestyle. I walk every morning with my dogs, and during the walk we practice virtually all of the exercises, making a game of it. That way, it keeps all of us on our toes. Around the house, our dogs have to sit and wait before entering or leaving, before eating, and before getting any extra treats (which they often get!). I routinely call them from the yard and reward them with their dinner or a treat, so I can be sure that they'll come when I call. If you consistently demand good manners from your dog, he'll gently slide into adulthood and old age, and you'll forget that he was ever an obnoxious adolescent!

Adulthood and Aging:

Two Years and Beyond

Part 3

Chapter Twelve

Choosing an Adult

Do you remember how long childhood and adolescence seemed? One summer day could last forever. When you reached adulthood and looked back on your youth, though, you realized that it lasted but a minute. This is also true of dogs. In most cases, if you can make it through the first two and a half years, you can relax. The dog you have raised will be the dog you have for many years. Most dogs live until they're 12, 13, or 14 years old, and some live even longer. If you've done your work well, you should get a great deal of enjoyment out of those years.

THE RIGHT ADULT FOR YOU

If you're considering adopting a dog older than two and a half or three years old, you should be quite selective—even more so than you were with puppies or adolescents. This is because at this age, most behaviors are somewhat entrenched, just as ours are when we are mature. Consequently, you're not as likely to be able to modify a dog's behavior in any meaningful way unless you're willing to devote a great deal of time and effort to the process.

Once again, try not to be taken in by looks. Some of the cutest dogs are not the best family dogs. On the other hand, some rather homely-looking dogs fit into a family beautifully. An adult dog is much more likely to be housetrained, is much less likely to be destructive, and is not going to need quite as much exercise as a younger dog. Of course, there are adult dogs who are not housetrained, who are very destructive, and who need lots of exercise every day. When you evaluate an older dog, then, try to employ the same selection process that you did with your younger dog. Separate him from the other dogs, and get to know him in a fairly quiet location. Give yourself plenty of time to make your choice. I've seen people who just point at a dog and say "I'll take that one," as though they're picking out a TV. If you're not careful, you could be picking out a pet who will cause more chaos in your household than you ever anticipated.

Friendliness

The first thing to look for is affiliative behavior, otherwise known as friendliness. The dog should want to be with you, and he should enjoy being petted. If the dog you're considering appears to be aloof—if he investigates the environment, sniffs around the perimeter of a yard or room that you're in, and doesn't come back to check in with you, there is cause for concern. This trait is more important to check for with adult dogs than with pups or adolescents. Younger dogs haven't formed their full personalities yet and may not actually be aloof; they might simply be interested in the great wide world.

The other extreme can also be problematic. If the dog sticks to you like glue, pressing against your body or pawing at your legs or arms, that could be indicative of a problem. He may be a controller, or he may have separation anxiety—or both! What you should look for is a dog who seeks attention, seems to like it, and who doesn't panic if you get up and walk out of the area.

Friendliness is one of the first traits to look for when selecting an adult dog.

The "Shy" Dog

Several years ago, I was asked to evaluate a dog whom our animal care technicians thought was shy. He remained in the back of his run and didn't come forward to greet them as did the other dogs. When I opened the door, he came willingly and allowed me to put the leash on. I then went into the tiny testing room we had at that time. Trailing me were three brand-new volunteers who also went into the room. It was my habit at that time to drop the leash to better observe the dog's interaction with people. This was a big mistake. The dog—a sexually intact Doberman/Shepherd mix—wasn't shy at all. He was aloof.

Once the dog was out of the run, he didn't even bother to look at me. Instead, he checked out every exit in the room (there were four of them) and urinated on each one. Then he glanced back at me, and the look he gave me sent shivers down my back. I sent my volunteers out of the room and slowly reached for his leash. I never even saw him lunge, but suddenly my hand was bleeding and he was staring at me again. I recovered my wandering wits and walked to the door, which I opened for him. As he walked through it, I closed it gently on him and picked up the leash. With that accomplished, I could put him back in the kennel.

This story serves as a lesson and a reminder that a dog who may appear shy might actually be aloof, a potentially dangerous trait in a pet.

Handling

Ease of handling goes right along with friendliness. The dog should allow you to touch him wherever you wish to. This means if you'd like to handle his feet you can, and if you want to look his teeth, that should be okay with him too. I can't emphasize this enough. There will be times when you need to dry him off, clean his ears, or clip his nails. Often, I've heard people say "He doesn't like it when I do that." Well, your child may not have liked it when you bathed her, but she had to accept it. You need to have access to your dog whenever you want to and in whatever way you want to. When we test for adoption suitability, we even hug a dog—just to make sure that we can.

Ease of handling is very important in your potential dog; he should allow you to touch him wherever you wish.

Food and Toy Guarding

Some dogs make it all the way to adulthood without ever learning to share. These dogs don't usually make great family members because you don't know what they will guard—it could be food, a toy, or even you. Some dogs only guard food or toys from other dogs, some dogs guard from everyone, and some will bite very hard indeed. If the place from which you're getting your dog does not test for food and toy guarding, consider doing so yourself. However, you need to keep yourself safe. Make sure that the dog is on a leash attached to something secure before you offer him some food in a bowl. Step away and allow him to begin eating. As he eats, approach him slowly. Watch his body language. If he looks up at you and wags his tail, you can continue to approach. If he eats much faster or stiffens and hovers over the bowl, stop approaching. And certainly if he growls, stop approaching. I don't usually recommend putting your hand into his bowl, as that could be dangerous. You can go through the same process with some kind of valuable chew toy, like a Nylabone. We use rawhide chews or pigs' ears, which tend to be prized possessions.

Many of my clients have excused their dog's behavior based on the fact that it's natural for a dog to want to protect his food or toys. They're right, of course. Imagine you are in a restaurant, and a waiter started taking your food before you were ready. Most people would chastise the waiter, and some people would become mildly angry. However, it would be completely inappropriate for you to stand up and punch the waiter in the nose! It is also completely inappropriate for a dog to bite his guardian over food or toys.

In any event, modifying food or toy guarding behavior can be dangerous and time consuming, especially with an adult dog. If you are not completely sold on this particular dog, I'd pass on him and consider another dog instead.

Dog-to-Dog Sociability

It goes without saying that most people do not want a dog who is aggressive toward other dogs. However, many people would like a dog who enjoys playing with other dogs. You can ask the owner or shelter whether the dog you're considering is sociable, or you can introduce the dog to another dog. Do remember that adult dogs often do not like other dogs until they are properly introduced, although they certainly shouldn't actively threaten other dogs. And even though a dog has been housed in a kennel with other dogs, it doesn't mean he is dog friendly. He and the other dogs may

CASE STUDY

CANINE INTERACTION

George had brought his three-year-old Lab to a consult because he was afraid Rex was getting aggressive. Rex had played at dog parks all his life, but lately he had gotten into a couple of fights. When questioned, George said that Rex had always played roughly—he loved to slam into other dogs and mount them. Most of his pals played the same way. Apparently, Rex had attempted to play like that with a Collie mix, whose play style definitely did not include mounting and body slamming. The Collie snapped at Rex, who then snapped back, leading to a full-fledged fight (and the first of several). Rex now didn't trust other dogs and tried to get them to back off when they approached him.

This could have been avoided if George had noticed that all dogs do not play alike. It could also have been avoided if George had monitored Rex a bit more assiduously. Because Rex was now an adult, we were going to have to work much harder to rehabilitate him.

be experiencing the "elevator" syndrome. People in an elevator can be uncomfortably crowded, and they will generally turn toward the front and watch the door or the floor indicators. Just because they're close together doesn't mean these people like each other or get along with all other people. They just have a temporary truce to get through an experience that gives them too little personal space. One of the more interesting aspects of the elevator syndrome is that the people on one very rarely make eye contact, and if they do, it's fleeting and sometimes awkward. If eye contact is made, people on an elevator seem to feel a need to make conversation, which is also awkward. This phenomenon can be seen in dogs who are confined as well, although their "conversation" is conducted with body language.

With this in mind, proper introductions should be conducted in as large an area as possible so that the dogs do not feel too much pressure to be close together. Allow both dogs to sniff the perimeter of the area—what they're actually doing is checking each other out without appearing to do so. Using a 30-foot (9-m) line is often a good idea, as you can hold the end and let the middle part drag on the ground. The dog will not feel like he's on leash, but you'll have some control over him. Try very hard not to let one dog charge the other. This demonstrates extremely bad manners and invites a defensive response. If you're concerned about how the two dogs will interact, don't do it yourself. Find a good trainer or behavior consultant to help you.

If your new adult dog is sociable with other dogs, I suggest that you observe carefully how he plays. Dogs' play styles vary radically, and miscommunication can lead to fights. As I mentioned earlier, bully dogs can overwhelm other dogs, and they may unwittingly offend more gentle players. Herding dogs tend to stare at and stalk other dogs, causing much anxiety for the "target." Some adult dogs do not like to play with puppies at all, and they can be highly intolerant. In fact, many adult dogs have no need to play with other dogs except those they've been introduced to and like. After all, they're supposed to be *our* companions! I enjoy and strongly recommend going for hikes with friends and their dogs. That way, the dogs can interact with each other, but they don't have to if they don't want to. They can also explore the constantly changing environment.

WHAT TO EXPECT FROM AN ADULT ADOPTEE

Adult dogs tend to take a much longer time to adapt to a household than younger dogs. They have developed habits over time, and it will take time to form new ones. Some adult dogs were pushy and obnoxious in their previous homes, and they expect to play the same role in their new one. Others were overly disciplined and are fearful of making a mistake.

If you've acquired your dog from a rescue group or shelter, try not to fall into the trap of feeling sorry for him, even if you think that he's been abused. If a dog ducks his head when he's being petted, it doesn't necessarily indicate that he was struck or beaten. It may just mean that he is wary of a hand overhead. On the other hand, if he cringes or runs away when you pick up a stick or broom, you are justified in thinking something bad happened to him. And if he's fearful of certain people, then he either hasn't had any exposure to them (which, as we've discussed, is so important) or he's had poor experiences with them.

At any rate, spoiling him to make up for his beastly previous owners doesn't do a dog any good whatsoever, and it may make him feel as though you're his servant—which you definitely do not want. It's much better to be loving, caring, and matter-of-fact—this is his new home, and he'll get no abuse here! Do keep in mind that he needs a leader, and that leader has to be you. To that end, hand-feed him a portion of his meals, have him sleep in a place of your choice (not on your bed, at least at first!), and institute a regular exercise regimen. Remember that dogs are naturally active in the morning and evening hours, and use that to your advantage, especially if you work. An adult dog can sleep up to 20 hours a day, and you can encourage that to take place while you're at work.

I also recommend strongly that you immediately begin to teach him that he'll have to be alone sometimes. People often adopt their new dog when they are on vacation and will have time to devote to their new friend. This is a good idea, but you must prepare your dog for the realization that it won't be this way forever. From the day you get him home, then, teach him that he can be alone, and show that you will come back by separating him from you several times daily for fairly short periods. I've had several clients whose dogs "acted out" in some way on Mondays only—chewing, digging, or trying to escape the house or yard. As you might guess, these behaviors occurred because the owners had their dogs with them constantly on the weekend, and the dogs became anxious when the workweek started. When you do leave your new dog, don't give him the run of the house, as he may just explore it in ways you don't want.

If you have another dog already, make sure that your new dog is sociable.

When setting household rules, make sure that all of your family members agree on what they will be, or they won't work properly. Either your dog will try to take advantage of one person, or he will become confused and insecure. Sometimes inconsistent families can actually cause major problems.

CASE STUDY

CONSISTENT LEADERSHIP

The Smith household had four members: husband, wife, a 19-year-old son, and an 18-year-old daughter. They had adopted a female adult Shepherd cross from a shelter about a year before I saw them. The male members of the family were large and powerful, and when Roxie did something they didn't like, they would physically reprimand her. To maintain their leadership role, they would pin Roxie to the ground and stare at her until she urinated in submission. (They'd learned this technique from a book they'd read.)

The two female members of the family were sweet and not nearly as large as the males. When Roxie did something wrong, they'd try to reprimand her, but both of them were actually frightened of the dog. They had good reason to be—Roxie dominated them. She wouldn't let them up stairs, through doorways, or even in the kitchen if she was there. She occasionally growled when they tried to pet her, and she had bitten both of them numerous times.

By the time I saw them, the family was totally dysfunctional and Roxie was actively dangerous. The husband and son blamed the wife and daughter for not being strong leaders. Roxie believed her status was below the men and above the women in the family. She also used the same violent techniques on the two women that the men had used on her. This is one of the rare occasions when I actually became angry with my clients because they had essentially ruined a sound, stable dog with their inconsistent leadership, not to mention causing injuries to two very nice women. Because she was dangerous, Roxie was eventually put to sleep. The Smith family then adopted two puppies. Both of them later developed aggression problems as well, all because the family refused to provide consistent leadership.

REACHING THE ADULT DOG'S POTENTIAL— AND STAYING THERE

I ran into a friend of mine the other day. As we chatted about our kids, she brought up her dog (as people are wont to do if they know me). Her Boxer is four years old now, and as she put it, "the neighborhood dog." She said that all of the neighborhood kids want to play with him, and he's a very easy dog to live with. After a few minutes, though, she mentioned how difficult it had been to get him to this point. He'd been a very obnoxious adolescent; she'd used my services on several occasions and had been through several classes. My friend acknowledged that if she'd known what a pain he would be in the beginning, she might not have gotten him to begin with. But all in all, he was worth it!

As we know, it can take a lot of perseverance to help your young dog (or your child) live up to his potential. Once training is completed, there's a huge temptation to rest on your laurels and just expect your pet to exhibit delightful behavior for the rest of his life. This is actually reasonable, especially if you maintain training and exercise programs to help him stay well and happy. Your dog doesn't jump on the counters or on visitors anymore. He doesn't dislocate your shoulder on a regular basis, and he's reliable at night. Every once in a while, he rolls in something disgusting just to remind you that he's a dog. But by and large, you feel— justifiably—that you can relax.

Your new adult dog needs you to be his leader.

However, one of the primary rules of behavior is that it isn't static. Behavior always changes. Things happen. When they do, you learn from them, your child learns from them, and so does your dog. He can be learning good things or bad things, but he does learn and remember them, and we must be aware of that. For instance, imagine you're on a walk with your dog when another dog attacks him. The attacking dog is black. After a quick tussle, the dogs stop fighting, with no harm done. However, the next time you see a black dog on your walk, your dog growls and lunges at him. In only one episode, your smart dog learned that black dogs are unreliable and possibly aggressive. This "lightbulb learning"

❖ Adult dogs are more vested in their behaviors than are puppies and adolescents—what you see is what you get—so evaluating their personalities is even more important than with younger animals.

❖ Once you get your dog home, you should set up a reliable routine quickly, including leaving your dog for brief periods so that he doesn't panic when you're not around.

❖ Training your adult dog is just as important as training your youngster because the only reliable characteristic about behavior is that it can always change.

can take place at any time in the dog's life, even when the dog is old. A trauma usually impacts a younger dog more dramatically than it does an older dog, but all dogs are affected.

Remember, your job is not done. Your dog will remain your two- to three-year-old child for the rest of his life, and you'll need to expect that. Thus, you'll need to ensure that he stays safe and he doesn't train himself to do things that you really don't like.

Chapter Thirteen

The Bigger Family: Multiple-Dog Households

Many people have more than one dog and have no problems at all. Some people get a second dog, and a world of trouble accompanies his arrival. Much depends on your choice of second dog and how you treat them both. This chapter is all about setting yourself up for success.

INTRODUCING A NEW DOG

There's an old saying about human families that applies just as nicely to canine ones: The only family in which there is no sibling rivalry is when there are no siblings. Some dogs just love all other dogs, but many are picky. If you have a dog (or two) and are planning to add another, you should know that problems could occur, especially if your resident dog is an adult and you plan to introduce another adult.

Consider the Opposite Sex

If you're still in the selection stage, consider getting a dog of the opposite sex. They're likely to get along with each other. It can be a bit more problematic with same-sex dogs, especially if they're close to the same age and temperament. Dogs live by rules, and status within your family can be very important. If two dogs keep vying for the spot right under you, there can be clashes.

Consider Personality Differences

I find that it's much easier on the guardian if the dogs in a family are not too similar in personality. If both (or three) dogs want the same thing at the same time, you're setting yourself and your canine family up for conflict. If they have different desires and different energy levels, they won't be competing with each other, which will help keep peace in your pack.

Consider Age Disparity

It's generally not a good idea to get a very young dog when you have a very old dog. Many people do that, thinking that the youngster will liven up the oldster, as well as prepare themselves and their families for the passing of the older dog. Sometimes the older dog does come to life, but just as often the older dog becomes depressed. There can be an age spread of several years, just not too many. It's hard to be specific because some dogs live so much longer than others, so you'll have to use your best judgment.

Consider Introductions in Stages

When you've made your choice, consider taking the introductory process in stages if possible—especially with same-sex dogs. Introduce the dogs several times in neutral locations before you bring them into your house. Taking a walk with both (or all) dogs is a great way to introduce them, as they will not have to pay attention to each other and can instead check out the environment. When you do bring them into your house, do so after a walk, when they are tired.

JEALOUSY ISSUES

Often a resident dog will get along just fine with a new dog until he realizes that his new friend is actually coming in! Like a child who doesn't really want to share her toys or her mother's affection, a dog is likely to show jealousy very quickly. Thus, you'll need to set house rules quickly and clearly. The dogs are most likely to collide over your attention, so it's important for your first dog to realize that the arrival of the new dog does not reduce the amount of attention the resident gets. If the new dog approaches you for petting and your resident tries to get some attention too, by all means give it to both of them. Make sure that each of them knows where you want them to sleep, and see that they both get all the food they need—but don't leave food down, as it's a possible source of conflict. I find it helpful to remove all toys for at least the first few days to eliminate any possible problems there.

To prevent problems, it may be best to add a second dog who is somewhat similar in age to your first dog.

THE NEED FOR EXERCISE

During the first three weeks, it's important to exercise the dogs a great deal—more than you might ordinarily do. The reason is fairly obvious: A tired dog tends to be a good dog. In addition, it can help forge a bond between your two dogs. Some dogs chase each other around a yard endlessly, which gets you off the hook much of the time. However, other dogs use a backyard as a giant bedroom.

Introducing a Cat to Your Dog

Take a great deal of care when you introduce a cat to your dog. The trick in this case is to give the cat all of the control. I find it helpful to put the dog on a tie-down, making sure that he is comfortable and has something nice to chew on, like a Nylabone. When you bring the cat in, give her a high location from which to watch the dog. She should be given time to observe him for several hours off and on before you ever actually attempt to introduce them. Cats take much longer than dogs to acclimate to new situations. It's extremely important that the dog not be given a chance to chase the cat—that's just too much fun! Sometimes even a somewhat predatory dog can live happily with a cat, as long as you prevent the chase.

Those dogs need to be taken out and walked or run—sometimes for several miles (km), depending on their age. Trips to a beach or careful use of a dog park are also appropriate. Do be careful, though, that they don't go after other dogs or chase them.

LEARNING TO BE ALONE

Another important consideration is teaching each of the dogs to be alone. They'll need to be alone at some point or another, and the longer you delay, the more difficult the process will be. I like my dogs to be bonded first to me and secondly to each other. Therefore, I separate them at least once a day for a couple of hours or so. You can have them sleep in their crates, you can put one outside and have one inside, or you can just close them into different rooms. This also helps the training process, which with two dogs can be an exercise in frustration. When you do train, set yourself up for success, and don't try to teach both of them at the same time. Some of our clients who have two dogs enroll both in the same class. That doesn't usually work out, as the dogs often try to get to each other from across the training area and sometimes bark and disturb the other clients. (We actually run a "Twofers" class geared for owners of multiple dogs—it's a great class, but it requires that both dogs already know their basic skills.)

Although two dogs can be great company for each other, they can also get into double the trouble, especially if they bond with each other and reduce their need for you. Facilitated behavior (pack behavior) can be a big problem in a variety of ways. For instance, it might be a lot of fun for one dog to charge fences or to chase cars. Add another dog, and the enjoyment factor can go sky high! Two dogs will also make each other braver—if one dog tends to growl or bark at a guest or intruder, two dogs may go further. It can be difficult to control two dogs at the best of times, and it can get downright infuriating at other times, when they both try to barge through the door or get in and out of the car.

THE KEY TO MANAGEMENT

The key to managing two dogs is environmental control and leadership. As I mentioned, you must make sure that the dogs need you more than each other so that they'll have a tendency to want to please you (or at least avoid your displeasure). Requiring both of them to sit before anything they want is very helpful, including getting into the car. I suggest having a place to put them when someone comes to the door (a bedroom or laundry room) to prevent doorway problems. The best time to train is not when a friend or stranger comes to the door. And calling them both to you immediately if they charge at the fence is a good way to handle that. Remember to praise them for coming, even if you're not pleased with them. They're not responding to the barking; they're responding to your cue to come to you.

If one dog seems to take on the rule of canine leader, you can lightly reinforce him by allowing him to go through doorways first (if he feels the need) and possibly petting him first. But by and large, your behavior should be that of a mother to her two small children. You should be so far above them that you don't really care who gets the bigger dessert. Actually, I've always played a treat-earning game

Consider taking the introductory process in stages if possible—especially with same-sex dogs.

CASE STUDY

KEEPING THE PEACE

Carrie had an Australian Shepherd named Sandy and a Lab mix named Bob. Sandy was typical of Aussies in some ways. She was bossy and pushy—bossy in that whatever Bob had, Sandy wanted (and got) and pushy in the amount of attention she sought from Carrie, especially if Bob wanted some too. Thus, if Bob asked for petting by placing his head on Carrie's knee, Sandy tried to push Bob out of the way and would literally lift Carrie's hand to get some petting. Luckily, Bob was an easygoing fellow and never took offense, so they had a peaceful family life.

Unfortunately, Bob died, and Carrie decided to get another dog. She picked a male Australian Shepherd. A charming dog, Roy had a lot in common with Sandy; he liked attention—lots of it—and was demanding about getting it. He also thought he should get his share of food and toys. So he was not pleased when Sandy tried to take things from him. By the time I saw them, they had had several tiffs, with lots of noise and no serious damage. Sandy has never taken to Roy, although Roy wouldn't mind playing with her. She growls when he comes close and seems to think he's out to get her stuff and her owner. Through management and some tough love, Carrie has managed to keep the peace, but it's precarious and I'm not sure it will last. The big mistake on Carrie's part was picking Roy to join the family. Although he's a male and a great dog, his temperament is too similar to Sandy's, and they constantly compete for the same resources. They're a disaster just waiting to happen.

with my dogs. I'll call "Cookies," and of course they all come running. The fastest one to sit gets the treat first. If there's an obvious leader who's a bit insecure (insecure leaders seem to feel that they have to keep asserting their leadership by posturing or guarding their own things carefully), then you can give him one first and last so that he doesn't feel deprived.

Our Rottweiler, Barney, was very insecure. He insisted on entering and exiting first, and he had so much dignity he couldn't even allow himself to play ball if another dog was present. He would make a move toward the ball, then seem to notice what he was doing and stop. The other dogs, Jobear and Ariel, would stand

back respectfully until Barney decided what he would do. They'd chase the ball after Barney strutted back to my side. If at any point he wanted the ball, they'd obligingly drop it. When we went for walks, he'd strut toward oncoming dogs and prepare to mount them, ready to bring them into his royal family. Unfortunately for him, the ultimate leader (me) never allowed this behavior. Barney was essentially a benign leader dog, though, and there were never any disputes with the other dogs. I did worry occasionally, especially with regard to my vehicle. As the leader, Barney felt he should get in first. However, if he did, Jobear wouldn't get in (as it was now Barney's territory). As a result, he had to be taught to jump in after Jobear. Then they both had to turn around, lie down, and be reinforced for being so "good." I go through this process even with other dogs because it tends to diffuse any problems before they begin. I certainly didn't want two Rottweilers to get into a fight in the back of my truck!

Chapter Fourteen

Activities for
the Adult Dog

People who play sports or who participate in other activities during their lifetime usually have a better chance of staying happy and healthy than those people who don't. Although your dog isn't going to join a gym, you can keep him healthy and prevent him from getting into trouble by keeping him busy with various activities and sports. They're great bonding tools because you have to do them together, and they provide wonderful exercise and stimulation.

There are many entertaining dog activities and sports from which to choose. All are helpful in entertaining your adult, and most are great ways for you to meet like-minded people. Agility, flyball, herding, jogging, lure coursing, rally obedience, retrieving games, and tracking are but a few. Some dogs are better suited to one activity or sport than another, as are their owners.

AGILITY

Agility is a competition that involves accuracy and time. Dogs are timed as they go through tunnels, jump over hurdles, and climb ramps. Most dogs appear to adore this sport, as do their owners. (The sport actually began in England as half-time

Agility is a timed race over an obstacle course.

entertainment at horse shows.) Herding dogs, like Border Collies, Australian Shepherds, and Shelties, tend to excel at this sport, but virtually all dogs can do it. They just need to be healthy and in good shape. Owners tend to get in good shape too, as you have to run through the course with your dog. By the way, agility doesn't have to be competitive—many people just enjoy the process.

FLYBALL

Flyball is an exciting, highly competitive sport. It's basically a relay race during which dogs fly over hurdles, grab a ball from a backboard, and fly back over the hurdles again. Unlike agility, which the dog can master fairly quickly, flyball takes a lot of preparation time and very dedicated owners.

HERDING

Herding is a fantastic sport that spotlights one of a dog's primary functions: herding sheep, cows, or even geese! Herding dogs are still used extensively on farms, and this sport shows just how it's done. Many herding dogs have a natural aptitude for this task, and engaging in this sport might just be a matter of pointing them in the right direction and keeping them from being too enthusiastic. I tried herding with my Belgian Tervuren, Ariel, when she was young. I was all fired up about using her instincts properly and helping her learn a whole new set of behaviors. Ariel, unfortunately, had other ideas. The sheep intimidated her, and she adroitly avoided them. On the other hand, she really enjoyed their waste products. I then tried herding with my Rottie Jobear, whom I'd brought with me just for companionship. He thought the whole thing was very interesting but seemed to want to get too close to the sheep. I could feel him thinking about mutton, and so I had to take him out of the ring.

JOGGING, RUNNING, AND WALKING

Many people like to walk, jog, or run with their dogs. It's a wonderful way to keep both of you in shape. There are just a few things you should know before you begin in earnest. First, very young dogs should not run for any length of time. It isn't good for their joints, which are still growing. There are varying recommendations, but by and large you shouldn't jog with your dog until he is nine months of age for light dogs and one year old for heavier ones. Check with your vet for more specifics on this. The other thing to keep in mind is the behavior of your dog and of other people. Some dogs—often particular breeds like herding breeds—revert to instinctual behavior when someone runs past them or when they run past a person. This means that they could nip before they think. With this in mind, give other people a wide berth, whether you're jogging or the oncoming person is jogging. In addition, slowing down as you pass is very helpful. Joggers and cyclists seem not to think of dogs as sentient beings who might get startled, and so they sometimes whip past with barely a look. I find it helpful to always carry treats with me when I'm out with my dogs in an area where there aren't too many people. Then, whenever I pass anyone, whether it be a person with a dog, bicyclist, horseback rider, or runner, I give out treats immediately afterward. This will help your dog pay more attention to you than to the attraction. (It makes people think you're a great trainer too because your dogs are paying so much attention to you!) But the best advice when you feel a bit concerned about your dog's behavior on the road is to slow down and give yourself space.

Help your dog burn off excess energy by getting involved in a sport or activity together.

LURE COURSING

Lure coursing uses another instinct—that of chasing prey. Sighthounds excel at this, although other dogs can do very well too. The "lure" is dragged along the ground at a great rate of speed, and the dogs chase it. They're scored on enthusiasm, speed, and agility.

RALLY OBEDIENCE

Competition obedience is very popular, but the moves are too militaristic for some people. Rally obedience is more relaxed

CASE STUDY

THE IMPORTANCE OF GETTING ACTIVE

Fran and her family got their Border Collie after seeing *Babe*, the movie about a herding pig. The kids loved the idea of getting a dog from a movie and named her Babe. Little did they know what they were getting themselves in for. Border Collies are very intense, agile, and sometimes far too intelligent. During adolescence, Babe was a huge challenge—she was an escape artist par excellence, she could destroy a room in record time, especially if her people were out of the house, and she nipped the kids, their friends, bicyclers, and skateboarders. The family had reluctantly come to the conclusion that their dog belonged on a farm, so they were planning to give her up when they returned from a consult.

Unfortunately, there are far more dogs who should live on a farm than there are farms, and Babe's future wasn't all that bright. They decided to give her one last chance, and one of my recommendations was to get her involved in a sport. Herding might have been the best choice for Babe, but the family didn't live in the country. Instead, they found an agility teacher and took Babe for some lessons. She showed a tremendous aptitude for it, and so did the 12-year-old daughter. They now compete in agility trials, but more importantly, the family was able to keep Babe.

and fun and a little less competitive (although that's changing). The handler and dog have to walk a course and stop at various stations, obeying signs like "U-turn," "down," and "stay." The dogs can be rewarded with praise and tend to be very enthusiastic.

RETRIEVING GAMES

Retrieving isn't just a game—it's a bonding tool, an exercising tool, and a training tool. Most dogs can learn to retrieve because it's a natural activity for them. However, we want our dogs to learn to retrieve only the items we want them to. To that end, we often punish them for picking up and playing with "non-doggy" items. Unfortunately, this type of behavior modification method can stifle or completely eliminate the retrieving instinct in your dog, or he may learn to play keep-away

Most dogs can learn to retrieve because it's a natural activity for them.

from you—he may learn that carrying things around causes you to pay attention to him or that bringing them to you to admire is downright dangerous. He may also learn that his own toys are boring (because you don't want to play with them) and your toys are valuable (because you don't want him to have them).

To teach your dog to retrieve, you first need to praise him for picking things up in his mouth, much as it might go against your instincts. If you praise him enthusiastically, he'll bring the item to you rather than running away from you. If it's an item you don't care about or that you want him to have, tell him he's a genius. If it's a forbidden object (and it's not dangerous or too fragile), praise him anyway. Then trade what he has in his mouth with another toy or a treat. Make sure that he believes that the traded object is just as exciting as the original—play with him, don't just hand it to him. Before long, your dog will bring you all sorts of things, and you won't

Now we can extend "carrying" to "retrieving" what you want! Follow the steps below: They're fun, and the process usually works.

1. Start out with a tug toy. It can be anything that allows you to hold onto one end and the dog to another. A soft flying disc will do, or a rope toy, like a Nylabone. If your dog won't play tug with you, you'll have to build that behavior, which shouldn't be too hard as most dogs enjoy it. (This can be accomplished by offering the toy and letting him tug it away from you over and over. Very few dogs can turn that down.)

2. Play tug energetically for a few minutes—do not win! That is, never be successful in

pulling the tug away from the dog. The dog has to win every time. When he is fully engaged and enjoying the game, stop playing and let the tug drop to the ground. If he picks it up and offers it to you, begin to play again. If not, pick it up with him. You have to demonstrate that without you, the game isn't any fun. Keep in mind that you never actually compete with the dog for the tug. Instead, if he starts to pull really hard, drop it and wait for him to come back for more.

3. Resume play. Now if he drops it or lets it go, pick it up and throw it about 2 feet (0.5 m). If the dog gets it and brings it back to you for more, that's great! Play tug with him again. If he doesn't get it, go to the tug with him, pick it up, and play again. Then it's tug, tug, tug, throw, retrieve.

4. Keep playing. Each time you get the tug or it drops, pick it up and toss it. You should be able to throw it a bit farther as time goes on. In many cases, you can start throwing it farther within just a few minutes. Each time, the dog should bring it back to you, or you can go to it and play with it and the dog. Don't ever take the dog's mouth off the tug; this action has to be totally voluntary. Also, don't reach for the tug in his mouth. He should offer it to you. If he lets you grab it and then wants to shake and kill it, let it go and wait until he finishes. He'll most likely give it you, and you can start the game again. Within a couple of sessions, he'll begin to realize that the retrieve is just as much fun as the tug, and he'll start giving you the tug toy instead of trying to take it from you.

Most dogs enjoy playing tug.

5. After a time, start using different tug toys to generalize the behavior. Perhaps go from a rope toy to a bumper or a flying disc. If you want to graduate to a ball, try getting

a rope ball first, switching to a regular ball as he gets more enthusiastic about the game.

6. Begin to throw the item farther and farther each time. Always end the game when he still wants to play.

Here's a tip if things aren't going quite right. Use two tugs—pick one up if he starts to run away with the other, and play with that one. Run around a lot! Use up those calories! If you're not excited, why should he get excited? When he trots toward you, entice him to play with your tug. Chances are he'll drop his (which is no longer interesting) and play with yours.

Some dogs learn to play in just one session. Other dogs take longer, but for most it can be taught within a week. That's a very short time to learn a very complicated chain of behaviors.

Tracking uses a dog's extraordinary sense of smell to find various articles on a trail or track.

CHECKLIST

❖ Take time to teach, and make sure that you know what you want to teach. Because dogs are nonverbal, they can become confused easily.

❖ Manage your dog's environment so that he is not practicing bad behavior while you're teaching good behavior.

❖ Be as consistent as you possibly can with behaviors and with cues. Remember that a bad behavior will stick around if everyone isn't clear about not accepting it.

TRACKING

Tracking uses a dog's extraordinary sense of smell. Owners and handlers lay a trail or track, and the dogs have to follow the track and find an article at the end of it. It's actually very easy to teach, just difficult when you get to the competition end. A new sport known as "nose work" is just emerging, where dogs learn to differentiate different scents from one another. It's very interesting, it uses the dogs' natural talent, and they seem to love it!

If you'd like to participate in a dog sport but don't know which one is right for you and your pet, you can enroll in dog "sport camps," where most of the sports in this chapter are taught. It's a great way for both of you to meet new friends as well.

Chapter Fifteen

Aging-Related Issues

As your dog ages, he will begin to slow down. His management and exercise needs will be reduced, and he'll tend to sleep even more than he did as an adult. Most older dogs do just fine with one walk a day to provide the stimulation they still need. They're often even more affectionate than they were in the past, and caring for an older dog can be fulfilling for both of you. However, you should be prepared to deal with some aging-related issues that may affect your dog.

HEALTH PROBLEMS

Like people, dogs suffer from more health problems as they age. I'm not going to attempt to cover the myriad health problems that dogs can have, but certainly arthritis and other joint problems are common, just as they are with humans. Sometimes older dogs even become incontinent, which can lead to extensive management problems. However, we often overlook health problems when it comes to our dogs' behavior. This is usually because dogs are stoic, unlike children, who are all too willing to share their pain. A dog might limp or cry when you touch a certain spot, but generally he's quite willing to keep chasing the ball despite being injured. A limp is obvious. However, internal problems aren't, and your dog is incapable of telling you exactly where it hurts.

When our Rottie, Jobear, was about nine, he suddenly and inexplicably refused to get into my vehicle when I was leaving work one day. I had a Ford Explorer Sport Trac, and like most SUVs, it was high off the ground. Jobear had never had any difficulty before, and it was surprising when he just refused to get in. It also caused a big problem—Jobear was about 120 pounds (54.5 kg), and I couldn't lift him. It was late, and there was no one else around. After I put the tailgate down, which is how he always jumped into the vehicle, he wouldn't get into the front of the car, even though it would have been easier. After an hour of cajoling, pushing, and pulling, I finally admitted defeat. I called my husband, who drove up to the shelter, and we then lifted him into the vehicle. Immediately thereafter, I ordered a foam step from a gymnastics supplier, and he used that to get in and out of the SUV for the rest of his life. Some people prefer ramps, but Jobear didn't, and the step was light and easy on my joints! (A veterinarian friend of mine subsequently told me that SUVs were responsible for many premature joint problems in dogs.)

The Link to Problem Behaviors

It's important to remember that discomfort and pain can cause behavioral changes. The dog may become irritable or moody. In some cases, dogs in discomfort will become aggressive, especially if they're suffering from a sharp or intense pain. At age 12, my dog Ariel had problems getting up from her bed—she grumbled at me when I insisted, so I helped her up slowly and carefully.

By the way, we humans have pain-elicited aggression as well. Not too long ago, I tripped while getting out of my car, twisted my ankle, and skinned my knee. Not only was I in pain, I was also embarrassed—my husband and his employee were right there looking at me. When my husband tried to help me up,

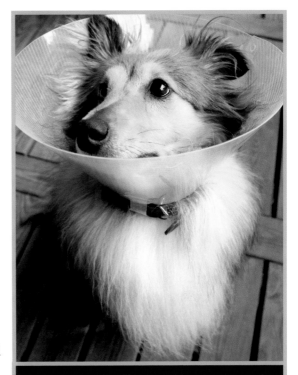

Like people, dogs suffer from more health problems as they age.

I responded by yelling at him and throwing keys in his general direction. This aggression was caused by pain, although it took a while and some rather profuse apologies for my husband to believe me.

Physical discomfort can also lead to other problem behaviors, ones that a little common sense can alleviate. One of my clients had a Basset Hound who suddenly refused to go down the steps to the yard and had begun defecating on the landing. His owners were furious, feeling as though this was some sort of act of defiance. When I pointed out that their dog was 15 years old and probably couldn't go down the stairs anymore, they were very embarrassed at their lack of sensitivity. They immediately got to work and built a ramp for the old guy, who responded by returning to his old habits and using his normal bathroom.

CASE STUDY

PAIN-INDUCED AGGRESSION

"Jeff" came into my office with his arm swathed in bandages. He didn't have his dog with him—he just wanted me to explain what had happened. He'd had his Golden Retriever, Max, from the time the dog was a puppy. The dog was a normal Golden: cheerful, compliant, and a nonstop retriever. Generally, Max slept very well—so well, in fact, that Jeff told me he had to grab Max's collar and drag him out every night to do his final business.

"Whenever I grabbed his collar, Max would growl at me," said Jeff. "He'd done that for years. I knew he'd never bite me."

This routine went on for about 12 years. Grab—growl—drag. One evening, Jeff grabbed Max, Max growled, Jeff pulled, and Max bit him. Hard. Enough so that Jeff had to go an emergency hospital and get multiple stitches.

"Of course I immediately had him put to sleep," Jeff said. "You can't have a dog around who will turn on you. I just want to know why he did it."

First of all, Max had been very patient with Jeff. In fact, he had been warning him to stop for 12 years! Secondly, Jeff hadn't noticed that Max was aging. All that ball playing had taken a huge toll on Max's joints, and he had serious arthritis. Instead of feeling a little uncomfortable when he was grabbed, Max was now hurting in his aging state. He didn't want to bite Jeff—he felt he had to.

Another aging problem behavior is increasing confusion or sometimes dementia. Some dogs will begin repetitive behaviors, often more intense varieties of their usual behaviors. Some dogs will demand bark more than they used to (bark to get what they want), while others will wander around and have trouble settling, especially in the evening. One of my friends' dogs has a route she takes every night—it drives my friend a bit crazy. Her dog goes out the dog door, walks around the yard for about a minute, and then stands at the sliding glass door, barking to come in. The poor girl doesn't realize that she can go back in the dog door. The solution to this? After the first time she does it, my friend closes the dog door. Her dog then stares at the door, looks confused, lies down, and goes to sleep!

Some dogs will go to a corner and seem to stare at it until their owners take them away. In this case, leashing the dog and tying it to a handy piece of furniture is a solution. You won't get anywhere by yelling at the dog or trying to train him out of it—it would be a bit like trying to train your granddad.

THE KING IS OLD—LONG LIVE THE UPSTART

If you own more than one dog, age can make a huge difference in the dogs' relationship with one another, especially if the older dog was the dominant one in your family. Some older dogs graciously let another dog take over the top spot, but many do not. They're used to making decisions, like who gets to go out the door first, who eats first, and who gets the softest bed. If you've been a good leader, you've helped them figure this stuff out, but sometimes status changes within the family happen without our help.

When the younger dog begins to make decisions, some pretty sticky situations may occur. I used to suggest that people let the dogs "work it out." I don't do that anymore because there's no guarantee that the dogs will come to an amicable agreement. Now I suggest that people get actively involved—in a nice way, of course. This is one problem that I have in my own household. Ariel, my Belgian Tervuren, is 12 as of this writing. Sophie, my Cairn Terrier, is nine years old. Sophie has always had a rather high opinion of herself, but over the last year she's been attempting to displace Ariel as top dog. There aren't many status-linked areas in our

Keep in mind that discomfort and pain can cause behavioral changes.

If you own more than one dog, age can make a huge difference in the dogs' relationship with one another.

household, so Sophie has had to work hard to find places where she can confront Ariel. As it is, Sophie follows Ariel when the older dog goes out to urinate, and she makes sure that she covers it completely. They occasionally have a "stare off" while lying in their beds under my desk. (I changed the configuration so that they can't do that anymore.) But problems have arisen when Ariel behaves in an uncharacteristic way and lies down on the floor in my office. (She usually curls up in her bed.) Then Sophie leaps into action. She stares into Ariel's eyes, and Ariel growls. Sophie growls back. The tension rises. There was one occasion where 20-pound (9-kg) Sophie actually got on top of 50-pound (22.5-kg) Ariel and growled down at her menacingly.

Unfortunately, I can't seem to take the whole thing seriously, and I tend to laugh when the scenario unfolds. This takes all the wind out of Sophie's sails, and she stomps out in disgust. This is exactly what I want. Anger exacerbates situations like this, whereas humor tends to help.

Overcoming Sibling Rivalry

There are other ways to help your older and younger dogs find peace. Exercise is very important, of course (as much as the older dog can take), and it should be exhausting for the younger dog. Encourage them to pay attention to you rather than to each other by playing retrieve or another game. Require that both of them sit politely for any sort of attention or food. Use tie-downs when they get chewies or

CASE STUDY

PLAYING THE BLAME GAME

Jeannette and John had two female Poodles, Amy and Jessie. When I saw them, Amy was ten years old with some arthritis setting in, and Jessie was a vibrant eight years old. Jeannette loved both of them, but she loved Amy best because she'd had her since she was a pup. Jessie had come to the household as an adult. Amy was the privileged one: She got to sleep on the owner's bed and sat between the couple when they were in the living room. Jessie was pushy and rough in play, but basically the two dogs got along well, with just the occasional scuffle. One day, they were playing in the living room and the play got out of hand. Jeannette scolded Jessie for playing too roughly, and Jessie promptly attacked Amy. After several minutes, Jeannette managed to get them apart, but Jessie had bitten Amy's ear. Jeannette put Jessie in the garage to "punish" her and then took Amy to the vet.

All went well for a couple of weeks, until one day Jessie took Amy's place on the couch. Jeannette scolded Jessie and pulled her off the couch, and once again Jessie attacked Amy. This time, more damage was done—to both dogs. Jeannette made an appointment to see me.

I found that both of these dogs were sweet, lovable animals, and the problem was actually Jeannette! Amy had been getting more arthritic, and Jessie felt the time had come to take the top spot. Amy was actually fine with that—she let Jessie go through doors first, and she didn't seem to mind if Jessie sat in "her" spot. But Jeannette did—she told me she would not give Jessie the privileges that belonged to Amy.

I saw them about six times and made all the suggestions that I could. But the fights kept happening—and escalating. Eventually, the two dogs had to be kept apart at all times, and the tension was almost unbearable. It seemed obvious that one dog would have to be rehomed, but Jeannette would have none of it.

The last time I visited Jeannette, the house looked like an armed camp. Each dog had her own tie-down, there were crates in the living room, muzzles hanging next to the leashes, and a kit to break up fights in every room. Amy still slept on the bed. The tragic part of this story is that it needn't have happened—if Jeannette had been a good parent, she would have allowed Amy to quietly resign her position in the household, and Jessie would have taken her place. Much of the tension between the two dogs and between Jessie and Jeannette could have been prevented.

bones to eliminate competition, and remove the items before you let the dogs off the tie-downs. Most importantly, don't take one dog's side over the other. This is extremely difficult for us, but it's a vital concept. When children are arguing, good parents don't take sides; they just tell the kids to stop fighting, and they provide something else for them to do. It does no good to place blame on one individual. Blame just creates more jealousy and exacerbates other problems. In fact, it can cause a solvable problem to escalate viciously.

WHEN IT'S TIME

Dogs don't really live very long—approximately 12 to 14 years if we're lucky. Our job is to notice physical and mental changes as they occur and try to help our dogs be as comfortable as possible. One of the services that we can do for our dogs is to notice when they are not getting any joy from living and to help them pass on. If your dog is healthy and happy until the very end of his life, you are lucky—and so is he. However, that often doesn't happen. I have had many clients who have asked my help in determining when might be the right time. We know that it's our responsibility as the human being to make a decision that the dog can't, but it can be very difficult. You need to be objective and subjective at the same time: You need to be both parent and Supreme Being. If you think only of the dog and not how you'll miss him, it becomes easier. Some people wait until the dog can no longer eat. Others wait until he can't seem to work up any

CHECKLIST

❖ All dogs age, and some show more problems than others, both behavioral and physical. In fact, the two are inseparable, as physical problems cause behavioral ones.

❖ As your dog ages, watch for signs of pain, like inability to get into a vehicle or limping after jumping out of one, and slowness in getting up, especially in the morning. Make accommodations for him, like a ramp for your vehicle and patience with increased slowness.

❖ If your older dog is behaving oddly, instead of blaming it on him being "stubborn," look first into whether he's showing confusion or pain-elicited behavior.

❖ Be prepared to help a dog take his last journey. It's part of our responsibility as human caretakers.

energy to play. Some people wait far too long—perhaps they don't notice that their pet is deteriorating, or perhaps they are just willing their pet to get better.

Afterword

Parenting a dog can be hard work. When you have a dog, you are always communicating something to him, like affection, anxiety, anger, and fear. At times, owners may unwittingly demonstrate that they don't care by leaving their dog alone much of the time and ignoring him when they're home.

We adults think that we communicate through our verbal language, but in reality, we communicate through our body language and behavior. We sometimes lack empathy, a quality that our kids often have. What is it like to be only a few feet (m) tall, looking at the world's knees and ankles? Kids know. If you take a little time to put yourself in your dog's place, you might just change some of your behavior. Children don't like to be stared at, and neither do dogs. And kids don't like to be crowded, pushed, manipulated, or dragged, even though these things often happen to them. If we adults learned to respect kids and dogs, we'd probably have fewer problem behaviors with both! There are several million reported dog bites every year. An awful lot of them occur when a person thrusts a hand into a dog's personal space and the dog reacts too quickly. Many more bites occur when people hug dogs—something that most dogs hate. Dogs must be conditioned to accept our embraces and not regard them as threatening.

THE BEST FAMILY DOGS

The best family dogs are tolerant of all of our strange behaviors; they can learn to like being hugged, petted, and hauled around. But not all dogs who live with families are truly family dogs. I've had a good many clients who complained bitterly that they shouldn't have to work on their dog's behavior—the dog should obey, the dog shouldn't bark or growl, the dog should stick around the house, the dog shouldn't object to being handled, the dog should know the difference between a stranger and a friend without an introduction. (I love that one!) Each and every dog is an individual, with characteristics and a personality of his own. Each dog needs a parent, and it should be the person with whom the dog lives—not a dog walker, a trainer, or a doggy day care facility. Each dog needs a family, even if the family consists of one person and one dog. If the family is stable, the dog is more likely to be stable.

Good parenting makes for good dogs. There are some bad dogs out there (even more these days, as the wrong people are breeding for the wrong reasons), and many people shouldn't have dogs, just as many people shouldn't have children. Some people get their dog "for the kids," who don't hold up their end of the bargain. The dog then winds up living in the backyard; he's fed daily (often too much) but gets no stimulation, no attention, and no love. We see these dogs in shelters across the country: They are literally dying for love. Some people get a dog for the machismo of it—tough dogs for tough guys. Those dogs are often encouraged to behave badly. One of the saddest scenarios I see is played out in shelters daily: The kids have grown up and moved out, the adults want to travel, and their dog (a pet who has lived with them, loved them, and been part of their lives for six to ten years) is no longer wanted. Sometimes abandonment occurs, where the family leaves town and deserts the dog.

Sometimes dogs live with us for as long as children do and sometimes much longer than a spouse, given the divorce rate. It's a substantial commitment to love, cherish, and care for a canine companion for 14 years or so. So often, dogs just become part of our expectations of life—husband, wife, kids, house, car, and a dog. I don't mean to say that dogs are as important as your children or spouse (although for some people they are). They are just important in their own right.

IF IT DOESN'T WORK OUT

There are times when we unwittingly make a bad match. Our dog's personality just doesn't fit ours, try as we might. Perhaps you got a Border Collie, not realizing that he might have an insatiable desire to herd things and that he needs about 5 to 10 miles (8 to 16 km) of stimulating exercise each and every day. Or maybe you really do have to move overseas, or a parent dies, leaving a pet without a home. What should you do?

Rehoming

The first thing I suggest is to try to find another home for your dog yourself and to use a shelter as a last resort. Some shelters are very nice, but most are still jails. They're generally underfunded and understaffed. They were created to handle surplus animals, and that's what most do. Dogs in shelters often go through something called "kennel stress," in which they slowly go crazy from understimulation. Even so-called "no-kill" shelters are often just places dogs go to die.

Newspaper Ads

You can put an ad in the paper to find your dog another home, but be careful because unscrupulous people have been known to acquire free dogs and sell them to laboratories. It's important to screen your applicants well.

Internet

Utilizing the Internet is also an option, though I'm not sure how truly useful this resource is. Even though many people will drive hundreds of miles (km) to pick up a dog whom they saw online, it's not at all clear what they'll get when they get there. As a consultant, I don't like to give specific advice online, by e-mail, or by phone because I have to actually meet the dog and his parents to understand a problem fully. I can't imagine acquiring a rescue dog simply by seeing a picture and reading a profile.

Breeders

Responsible breeders will generally take a dog back, even if some time has passed. At the very least, they should provide you with resources to help in rehoming. Good breeders will have you sign a contract saying that you will return the dog to them if you can't keep him. Unfortunately, many breeders are not as responsible as they should be—but it's worth the attempt.

Rescue Groups

Rescue groups can be an excellent resource for dogs. Most are for purebred dogs (created by responsible breeders and aficionados of a certain breed), but there are also many for mixed-breed dogs. One of the most important aspects of a breed rescue group is that it understands breed instincts and tendencies. It will know how to make an appropriate match for the breed. Some breeds are notoriously hard to place, many for good reason. For instance, not every family can provide a good home for a Chow or a Shiba Inu—they have very specific needs, and good breeders know that.

Shelters

If you've used all of the resources you can think of and a shelter is your only choice, then be realistic. In most parts of the country, there are far more pets than there are prospective owners. The older a dog is, the worse his chance of finding a home. And dogs with problem behaviors—even dogs who have housetraining issues—can be virtually impossible to place. Would you want a dog who is aggressive, eliminates in the house, or breaks out of any enclosure? It's tempting to blame the shelter for not being able to place a dog, but the reason shelters exist is because so many animals are unwanted. Believe me, we would much rather have empty runs because people breed responsibly and keep their dogs! Blaming a shelter is like blaming a jail for housing prisoners. All in all, it's so much better to choose wisely, raise your dog well, and keep him throughout his whole life.

WHY WE LOVE OUR CANINE KIDS

I think I love dogs because they are with us in the spiritual sense of the words. When I'm walking with my dogs, I need no one else. I'm listening to them, playing with them, and watching them (my favorite!). I enjoy the process of helping them grow from puppyhood, when they begin to learn the ways of the human world, through old age, when they slow down and need so much. When we have children, we often think years ahead. When they're tiny, we think about preschool. Later, as they get a little older, we think about elementary school, high school, college, and their eventual careers. Sometimes it's easy to forget to enjoy our children for who they are right now. Taking the time not only to teach them but to enjoy them is hugely important.

Learning how your dog communicates is loads of fun. I remember when I discovered that when a dog is looking hard for something, his tail goes up and wags ferociously, and when he finds whatever it is, his tail drops into its normal position. He is so obviously having fun, doing his version of shopping. I love to watch Ariel "stalk" Strider, only to suddenly pop out at him. I'm sure she's saying the canine equivalent of "Boo!" Dogs are so much like children yet so different as well. There's so much responsibility involved with raising both, but it's so worth it!

As I write this, I have my family's own three dogs, plus three others I'm watching. While six dogs are too many for me, it's entertaining to witness their similarities and differences. Two of the dogs are Cavalier King Charles Spaniels who belong to my mother-in-law. They're affectionate and very sweet. Their chief entertainment in life is following me and chasing after flying things, like bugs and birds. The other dog is a Corgi mix, a rescue who was attacked once while her owner was walking her. Now she's afraid of other dogs. On our walks, you can see her gathering up her courage to pass them. She always earns a reward for her bravery. The Cavaliers and Ariel, my Belgian Tervuren, were raised from puppies in the ways I described in the beginning section. The other dogs—Sophie the Cairn Terrier, Strider the German Shepherd, and Ruby the Corgi mix—were all rescues and will struggle with many of their problems for the rest of their lives. However, I've used many of the techniques described in this book to help them, and I believe I've been successful.

Owning a dog can be a wonderful, fulfilling experience. Most of it is up to us and how we deal with our dogs' training, growing stages, and problem behaviors. (May they always be small!) Dogs do need a lot of work, but just like kids, they're worth it!

Appendix:

Problem Behaviors

As a consultant for the last 15 years, I'm constantly amazed and awed by the dedication many owners display with regard to their dogs—even those with very serious issues. They truly think of their dogs as their children. Unfortunately, from puppyhood to old age, dogs can have a variety of problem behaviors. Some have just a few, while others have many. Some are minor, and some are serious. In this section, I've addressed some problem behaviors and provided some behavior modification techniques. Do remember that if your dog has serious issues, you should consult a knowledgeable and trustworthy personal consultant or trainer who will construct your own modification program based on your particular dog and your relationship with him.

BARKING

It's a fact that dogs bark. It's also our fault, inadvertently. Before dogs were domesticated, they were wolves, and wolves don't bark much. They have some specific bark signals, but they don't go on for hours and hours and hours, like your neighbor's dog. That dog may be barking for a wide variety of reasons, including a few we'll explore in depth.

Why Dogs Bark

Actually, barking is really a puppy behavior that has carried through into adulthood. Pups bark to tell their moms where they are, because they're having fun, because they're lonely, and because they like to bark. For adult dogs in the wild, survival is a pretty serious business, and there's no point in advertising one's whereabouts unless one is communicating something fairly important.

That said, most people, especially neighbors, don't like barking dogs, and it's up to us owners to do something about it. First, we have to figure out why the dog is barking. Is he lonely, frightened, bored, alarmed, frustrated, demanding, or overly happy? Listen carefully to the bark and you'll know. Lonely or frightened dogs will often howl as well as bark. Bored or frustrated dogs will bark repeatedly. Demanding dogs will stare at you and tell you what they want with rhythmic barking. ("I want in!") Happy dogs will bark while they're doing something like chasing another dog or playing ball. Alarm barking is exactly that: Your dog is telling someone or something to go away, or he's trying to tell you something is going on (but you're not responding appropriately). It's often a "woo-woo-woo" sound.

I often get calls about barking dogs, both from the dog owners and their neighbors. It's very frustrating being on the receiving end, especially when you're trying to sleep. Many owners don't know their dog barks during the day when they're gone, as they stop as soon as they hear the car coming down the street or into the driveway. If you've been getting complaints but just can't believe it's your dog, purchase a noise-activated recording device—you will soon find out. Sometimes the origin of the barking is actually somewhere else, and you can prove that it really isn't your dog. More often, you'll realize the barking is definitely a nuisance and that you'll need to address it.

Behavior Modification Methods

Once you've figured out that the barking is really coming from your dog and you understand why he is barking, you can address the problem.

Manage the Environment

One of the best ways to deal with a bored or lonely dog is to manage him and his environment. Exercise him extensively and when you leave him, position him in a place where he won't be overstimulated. Try to tire him out in the morning and evening hours when you're home and can exercise him so that he'll sleep during the middle of the day. Some dogs bark when they are in the house, oftentimes because they've found a perch from which to view the world and comment on it. Try eliminating the perch or closing draperies to manage his environment.

Use Your Leadership Skills

If your dog is alarm barking, you can don your "leadership" hat. The first few times your dog barks in the yard when you're home, go out, investigate like a good parent should, tell him everything is all right, and then bring him back into the house. Reward him when you get there—you want a dog who is happy to come in. After you've done this several times and found nothing amiss, refrain from going outside and just call him.

Reward for Quiet

If he's pretty dedicated about barking, you can use the following method. It's pretty dramatic and often works. You'll need to be close to your dog when he barks, and you'll need to have treats with you. When he barks, quickly move into him using your lower body while saying "Shhhh." When he stops, praise him, wait a couple of beats, and then give him a treat. In this case, it's important that you don't reward him immediately when he stops, as he could interpret that as reinforcement for his barking. The act of moving into him should interrupt the barking, allowing you to get your cue in.

Use the "Stupid Mom Routine"

If your dog demand barks—stands and looks at you expectantly while barking rhythmically—try the "Stupid Mom Routine" I mentioned earlier in the book. As soon as he starts, ask him if he wants to go outside (you can also ask him if he wants to go into the laundry room or other unpopular place), take him there, wait five seconds, then let him back in. Repeat as needed.

Keep Your Dog Occupied

When you do leave your dog, consider giving him a hard rubber toy stuffed with food to help him while away the hours and stimulate his brain. Although you can just stuff a hollow rubber toy with dried cookies or kibble, your dog is likely to get through the toy quickly and turn his attention elsewhere (like to a tasty rug). If you're a bit more creative, you'll occupy more of his time and give him a job. Here are a few ideas to get you started; the more creative you are, the happier your dog will be.

First, figure out if your dog likes to work for his food or if he gives up easily. You can stuff the toy with small food items that fall out with just a tiny bit of work and let him start with that. Then stuff one with some of the following ideas and see whether he will continue to work at the toy until all the food is out. You should prefer a hard worker, of course, as he'll spend lots more time trying to figure out how to get that food out of there!

Mixtures such as peanut butter, cream cheese, canned cheese, mashed potatoes, canned dog food, plain yogurt, cottage cheese, tofu, or toddler food can be used to bind smaller bits of food together. You can also use soft cheese cubes. Place the cubes in the hole, microwave the toy until the cheese is melted and then stuff some cookies in the mix. Cool thoroughly before giving it to your dog.

The following are some tips on how you can make the stuffed toy more challenging and exciting for your dog.

❖ Wrapping the stuffed toy in an old, clean diaper, tea towel, hand towel, or t-shirt and tying the ends off will create a puzzle for your dog. (Increase the level of difficulty as he graduates.)

❖ Enclosing the toy in an old oatmeal box, shoe box, margarine container, or other container that you don't mind being taken apart increases the puzzle aspect.

❖ Hiding the stuffed toy around the house or yard stimulates a dog's genetic hardwiring to hunt for his food. At first, hide the toy in rather obvious places and then gradually make him work harder to find it.

❖ Harder and advanced stuffing for the creative hunter in your home begins with plugging the small hole with peanut butter. Then add cookies, cubed meat, cooled chicken or beef broth, and freeze the toy into an icy treat. This should be given to dogs outside or in a room that can be cleaned easily because it can get messy.

For the really clever dog, layering the toy and sealing the big end of it is really challenging and can give him hours of doggy delights. Pack these as tightly as possible. The last piece in should be a sealer piece, such as a dried apricot, cheese ravioli, or tortellini.

- Layer 1 should be the deepest and can include anything of really high value, like freeze-dried liver bits.
- Layer 2 can contain anything you want—perhaps dog kibble, cookies, liver biscotti pieces, peanut butter, or dried banana chips.
- Layer 3 suggestions include baby carrot sticks (cut to the appropriate size so that your dog won't choke), celery, turkey, chicken, leftover meats, dried apples, or apricots.
- For dogs on a diet, you can substitute a crumbled rice cake, plain croutons, salt-free or fat-free cream cheese or peanut butter, tofu, or yogurt for the above ingredients.

ANXIETY

Dogs, like people, are social animals. I know I've mentioned this before, but it bears repeating because many problem behaviors that develop have to do with a lack of proper socialization during the months when your dog needs it the most (two to four months of age).

There are many physical signs of stress and anxiety, and the following are a few examples:

- dilated pupils
- dropped tail
- dry panting
- hair loss
- looking from side to side
- pacing
- penis crowning
- rigid posture
- stretching
- sweating from paws
- tail held under body
- tears pinned or twitching
- yawning

Why Dogs Become Anxious

Some dogs are just generally anxious, overreacting to stimuli that startle them—often spooking, barking, or panting, sometimes even lunging, snapping at, or biting what they fear. In addition to general anxiety, some dogs suffer from anxiety brought on by specific events. Many dogs become very anxious, for example, when a thunderstorm or windstorm is approaching. This anxiety can become so bad that the dog may become phobic and require major behavioral work to help him overcome his fears. Still another form of anxiety has to do with separation from the human family. These dogs tend to stick like glue to their owners when they are home. We'll discuss that one first.

Separation Anxiety

When your child was very young, you probably left her in the crib or at least you tried to. Babies don't want to be alone any more than dogs do. But it has to happen, sooner or later. I remember sitting outside my daughter's room, listening to her cry. Sometimes I'd even talk to her from the doorway, just to let her know I wasn't very far away. However, she had to learn to calm herself down, to relax and go to sleep. Dogs must do this too.

Separation anxiety is relatively easy to diagnose and very difficult to cure. A dog with separation anxiety will often try madly to get out when he is left alone. He'll dig at doors and windows in an effort to find his family, and he is likely to ignore his food while the owner is gone. Often, dogs with separation anxiety will drool for hours or lick their paws, causing the hair to become stiff from saliva. If they're really panicked, they might urinate and/or defecate in the house. They may bark and howl for hours, and some even cause injury to themselves in their efforts to get out and find their "mom" or "dad." They are panic stricken. Those owners who are unable to comprehend this behavior often think that their dog is being destructive because he's paying them back for leaving. As a result, they punish the dog, which only worsens the behavior. In many cases, confinement in a kennel or crate aggravates the problem, even though it can stop the destruction. However, these dogs may injure themselves trying to bite or dig through the bars, or they may take to biting or licking themselves compulsively.

Behavior Modification Method

Behavioral treatment involves working on your dog's emotions. He has to learn that you will come back, and he has to learn it in short, calm increments, beginning with just a few seconds of separation and working up to longer periods. Dogs can't learn much when they're hysterical—they need to be able to think. This means that owners have to learn to work within their dog's threshold as they try to encourage calm behavior.

Just as not all dogs are alike, there is no "one way" to cure separation anxiety. Some people find it helpful to leave their dog in a room where he can't see them come and go. You can even convince some dogs that you aren't leaving at all by placing clothing just outside the door. Others find that it helps to let their dog actually watch them leave and then watch them return. Still others find that ignoring the dog for 20 minutes or so before each departure helps keep the anxiety level down. Many people even use a "goodbye gift." This could be a random treat dispenser toy, or it could be something else your dog only gets when you're leaving.

No matter what, each arrival and departure should be cool and calm. When you do leave, pick a verbal cue that tells your dog what's happening. "I'll be right back" or "I'll be home soon" are fine choices. The first departures should be no more than 30 seconds, and they should be increased in slow increments, always at the threshold of your dog's anxiety. When you notice that he's getting more relaxed about your imminent departure, begin leaving for longer periods. If you're using the "goodbye gift," remember to pick it up as soon as you walk in the door. Try really hard to avoid long separations during this retraining program, or it won't work. If you have to leave your dog for extended periods, perhaps a doggy day care would be a good idea while you're going through the process. It's expensive but not as expensive as new doors or carpeting.

While you're practicing the leaving/returning routine, you can also teach your dog to be crated for various lengths of time. If he is panicked, crates are not recommended. As I mentioned previously, crates tend to increase panic—some dogs actually claw so much at the crate that their mouths and paws bleed. However, if he learns to like his crate, you'll be able to use it as time goes on.

Anti-anxiety medication can often help extreme separation anxiety. If you think your dog suffers from this problem to a great degree, consult your veterinarian for information. Even if your vet doesn't feel comfortable dispensing these kinds of prescriptions, she will probably refer you elsewhere.

Overall, remember that to modify the behavior of a dog with separation anxiety, you'll need to reduce the anxiety and teach your dog to be alone over a long period. Our rescued German Shepherd, Strider, is afflicted with this disorder—or perhaps we should say our family is! We've been working on the problem for as long as we've had him. I daresay he'll never be "cured," but we are better able to manage his problem now.

Separating Anxiety (Control Issues)

Some dogs just can't handle the separation process. Small children often have the same problem. You take your child to day care or preschool, for example, and she clings, cries, and basically throws a fit in order to make you stay. However, when you're out of sight, she calms down immediately. This, of course, is why day care teachers urge you to leave quickly! Some dogs will also throw a fit when you leave them. They will cry, whine, and sometimes attack your back as you try to exit your house. Once you're gone, they will settle down and go to sleep. You can tell if your dog has that form of anxiety if you sneak back after an hour or so and peek in the window. Dogs with separating anxiety are usually asleep or getting into mischief. They're not crying at the door.

Behavior Modification Method

This problem is much easier to solve than separation anxiety, and dogs usually respond to some training. One of my clients had a Parson Russell Terrier who lived up to his breed reputation. He was adopted, and the family—parents and one 12-year-old daughter—was on the verge of returning him to the shelter. He had begun leaping at them and biting at their clothes when they tried to leave the house. Then, after a few weeks of this behavior, he started getting agitated at earlier cues that indicated they were thinking about leaving the house. In fact, he started barking and whining when anyone picked up her purse/briefcase/school pack or jingled her keys. It got so bad that he would leap on them when they tried to take the garbage out and when they brushed their teeth in the morning (the final straw). This family loved the little guy, but all of their clothes had rips in them, and his teeth had brushed a butt a few times. After witnessing all of these symptoms of separating anxiety, when they finally got out of the house, he'd settle down and go to sleep!

We tried adjusting the dog's status by not allowing him on the sofa (where he virtually lived) and giving him attention only when he was asked to do something. Unfortunately, this didn't make much of an impact. We then tried mixing up cues. The family would get their work clothes on in the evening or take the trash out through the back door. Nothing worked—this guy was smart. Finally, we tried doorway training again, even though the family's earlier training at doors hadn't had any effect. This time we did it together. Each family member participated in the teaching of a *sit-stay* about 10 feet (3 m) back from the door. The reward was a treat tossed behind the dog so that he had to go back to get it upon being released. We did it first without opening the door, then proceeded to opening the door and standing in the threshold, then standing right outside the threshold, then 6 feet (2 m) away, then closing the door, and then closing the door and going to the car. This method worked, and it only took about half an hour to teach all six of these progressions. The family decided to keep the dog (and take some classes), and as far as I know, they still have him.

Doorway training is quite effective on dogs who don't want you to leave, and it can be pretty successful if you stick with it.

Generalized Anxiety

Some dogs are temperamentally sensitive, overreactive, and spooky. The sight or sound of something perfectly normal can make them cringe and shake in fear. For example, my Belgian Tervuren, Ariel, is very frightened of snapping noises. The sound of a knife on a cutting board sends her scurrying to her bed. She has been noise sensitive since she was a pup—in fact, it's something of a breed characteristic. If snapping noises happened all the time, I could have habituated her to the sound. However, they don't, so the behavior has remained.

Generally, overreactive dogs are more likely to spook when there is a sudden environmental change, especially if it's very quiet inside where they are and there's a sudden sharp noise. If your dog is in a busy, noisy environment, his chance of reacting by bolting or hiding is lessened considerably. If your dog is noise reactive, you'll need to make sure either the environment is under your control or he is under control (leashed or possibly crated).

Behavior Modification Method

The way I recommend helping these overly sensitive dogs is to associate an enjoyable behavior with the frightening sound. Whenever I'm around and a "snap" occurs, I call Ariel to me and praise and reward her. Sometimes that's not possible, in which case she usually hightails it for her bed, which is her "safe" spot. You can also flood a sensitive dog with other sounds, thus masking the scary noise. Calm music or white noise are often pretty effective.

Superstitious Behaviors

Yes, dogs can be superstitious, although not in the same way that humans are. Whereas a person might cross her fingers or wish upon a star, a dog is likely to think that one thing is inexorably attached to another. For instance, some dogs seem to think that if you tell them to sit, they're supposed to bark too. This is because their owners have inadvertently reinforced "bark" when they thought they were reinforcing the *sit*. This isn't a particularly difficult behavior to modify, but sometimes dogs can come up with doozies!

Most superstitious behaviors are amusing or frustrating at most, but they can be more than that. For instance, let's say your dog believes that every time you pick up your keys, he will be left alone. Because he doesn't like being left alone, he starts vocalizing. This is a problem! What he has done is attached the sound (keys) to an action (leaving), and even though you don't leave, he still responds as though you do.

Other superstitious behaviors might concern places. Just as a person who had a traumatic experience might associate the place it happened with the event itself, dogs can do the same. My own dog, Ariel, developed a superstitious behavior around a portion of the fire road on which we routinely walk. She was bitten by several yellow jackets, and it took me some time to remove them from her rather luxuriant coat. After that incident, whenever we'd pass that part of the trail, she'd panic, spin, and bite at her coat. I handled it by acting goofy and jogging past the place; after a while the association dimmed, although she was never completely comfortable at that spot.

Behavior Modification Method

To modify superstitious behaviors, only reinforce the behavior you want to see. For instance, each time you pick up your keys, give your dog a treat. Then the association will be keys=treat instead of keys=alone. If you were trying to change the sit/bark scenario, you'd have to wait patiently for a *sit* to occur without a bark and reinforce that behavior. After a bit, you could cue the *sit* but only reinforce it if there was no bark attached.

Phobias

Some superstitious behaviors can balloon into full phobias, where the dog is so frightened of an event or sound that he cannot cope with it. This can lead to massive destruction as well as self-mutilation because some dogs chew on their feet and legs to relieve their anxiety. Phobias are the same for dogs as they are for people: excessive fear associated with an event or experience. As you know, many people are afraid of heights or spiders. Phobic dogs (who are otherwise perfectly normal), on the other hand, tend to show extreme fear of noises, especially those that are loud and crackling. The fear begins with one event and escalates very quickly to terror.

Thunderstorm phobia is relatively common in some areas of the country where there are lots of storms. Many dogs show the same responses to fireworks (with the result that shelters all over the country receive hundreds more strays on July 4th and the day after). A terrified dog will do anything to get away from the sound. If he's inside, he'll try to get out, sometimes going through a window. If he's outside, he'll try to go inside, or he'll jump the fence to get out of his yard. A dog with thunderstorm phobia is a pitiful sight, running from place to place in the house, looking for somewhere the noise is not. Many of these dogs hide in bathtubs or next to pipes in basements. Some people theorize about "grounding" or some other physical reason why dogs do this.

Oftentimes, phobias develop later in life. In fact, it's one of the few problem behaviors that tend to develop over time. I have had several clients with dogs who spent their first few years accepting noises of all kinds but then later developed major problems as they reached middle age (six and up).

Behavior Modification Method

Whatever the cause of a dog's phobia, behavior modification is extremely difficult and usually involves extensive desensitization. I suggest that you see an experienced, reputable behaviorist or veterinarian to treat these problems. They may suggest the use of calming drugs while you work on the modification process.

Obsessive-Compulsive Disorders

People with obsessive-compulsive disorders tend to repeat a behavior, well, compulsively! A human with obsessive-compulsive disorder (OCD) might feel compelled to repeatedly wash her hands or pull her hair out. Once begun, it's very difficult for the person to stop the behavior. It's not known if dogs can develop the same kinds of obsessive-compulsive disorders as humans do, but they can definitely manifest compulsive behaviors, such as constant spinning or licking at the same place over and over. Sometimes compulsive behaviors are our fault. Take fly catching, for example. A dog might begin by snapping at flies, occasionally maybe even catching one. When the dog catches a fly, his owners laugh and encourage him. This is great attention, and some dogs will start air snapping even when there are no flies to catch. Then they get even more attention from the owners. After enough repetitions, voilà! You have a dog who can't stop catching flies. The obvious remedy in this type of situation is to pay no attention when your dog catches flies. Instead, pay attention when he exhibits a behavior you'd like to see repeated.

Behavior Modification Method

If your dog shows signs of obsessive-compulsive disorder, I suggest that you visit a professional. These behaviors can be very difficult to deal with. Generally, it may be helpful to try distracting the dog from the compulsion by training and reinforcing a different behavior. For instance, if your dog compulsively sucks his flanks (a behavior often seen in Doberman Pinschers), you could have him chew on a bone instead or chase a ball. Exhaustion almost always helps, so try to exercise him at least a couple of times a day.

General Behavior Modification Recommendations

There's a tremendous temptation to try to console the frightened dog—to cuddle and stroke him, murmuring "It's okay, honey." I know because I've done that myself. However, it doesn't really do a lot of good and may actually make matters worse.

Say your daughter falls down and scrapes her knee. What moms and dads usually do is to run to the child, give her a big hug, and depending on the age of the child, kiss it better. Then the child is urged to resume playing and forget the injury. This is precisely what you should do with minor fears or accidents that scare your dog. Pick up or hold the dog briefly, check for injury if it was an incident that caused the fear, and then begin to play a game with him. This will help him get over his trauma quickly. If you spend too much time comforting, your dog may well associate the fearful incident with a lot of attention from you. This can actually worsen the apparent fear or at least the aftereffects. Some children learn to seek "comforting" for the same reason.

Things get trickier with more serious fears or phobias. Modification methods for all of these problems involve changing the association from stimulus (e.g., noise)=fear to stimulus=pleasure. To do this, you should start on a program of desensitization and/or counterconditioning. I urge you to make sure that your dog is healthy first by visiting your veterinarian. If there's something physically wrong with your dog, then all the behavior modification in the world won't help.

Desensitization and Counterconditioning Techniques

Desensitization involves exposing a dog to the particular thing he's afraid of at a level that he can handle. Counterconditioning establishes a relationship between an event and something delicious or otherwise pleasant. I often use counterconditioning alone, as it's a fairly simple way my clients can help their dogs change their behavior. Desensitization takes longer and is almost always paired with counterconditioning because the combined behavior modification can work faster. I'm going to use an example of sound sensitivity as the behavior we will work on, just because it's easier to explain one specific behavior. However, you can use desensitization and counterconditioning on a wide variety of problem behaviors, including fear of people and other dogs.

Here's an example of using counterconditioning alone (creating an association between something scary and something good). My Cairn Terrier Sophie was riding in the front seat of the car with me when I had a minor accident—my side mirror sideswiped another car's mirror. The resultant "crack" sound was enough to traumatize anyone, and it certainly did Sophie. After that, although Sophie was happy to get into the car, she hid under the dashboard once she was aboard. Whenever there was even the smallest "crack" (a stone hitting the car, for example), I tossed her a tidbit. Over a period of time, Sophie seemed to expect the tidbit, and after several months, she began enjoying her car rides again. In fact, the noise itself became a cue for the tidbit. I imagine she began looking forward to cracking sounds!

Behavior modification becomes much more difficult and time consuming with severe emotional responses, like thunderstorm phobia, where you will have to combine desensitization and counterconditioning to get any real response.[1] Here's how that works. You expose your dog to the sound at a very low level for fairly long periods. (You can buy

---

[1] Even then, some phobic responses are too extreme to respond to behavior modification alone, and some dogs may need anti-anxiety medication.

CDs of sounds that tend to frighten dogs, including the sounds of thunder, fireworks, backfiring trucks, and motorcycles.) As the dog begins to accept the sound, make it louder and louder until finally it's quite loud. If when you play the sound you also give the dog a toy stuffed with food or some other kind of pleasant experience, you are adding counterconditioning, which will enhance the technique. Some dogs can't eat when they hear a noise that scares them. If you give food to him anyway, you'll know that your treatment is effective when he starts eating.

Unfortunately, desensitization and counterconditioning are not guaranteed. A behaviorist veterinarian friend of mine in the Midwest had his office wired to recreate the sound of thunder—he put speakers in the attic so that the sound was coming from the "sky." Then he started some of his clients on the program. What he found was the dogs learned to cope well in his office. But because dogs are place learners, in most cases the behavior modification didn't generalize to the real world.

AGGRESSION

Aggression is the number-one complaint about dog behavior. You hear "That dog is aggressive!" as though the one word describes it all. Of course it doesn't.

Imagine that your teenage daughter comes home from school, upset because one of her schoolmates criticized her loudly in front of a group of her friends. Your daughter is furious as well as hurt—she'd really like to punch that girl or at least give her a piece of her mind. The schoolmate behaved in an aggressive manner, and now your daughter is feeling aggressive too. Actually, your daughter was not being aggressive—she was behaving defensively when a schoolmate threatened her. The schoolmate was behaving in an offensive manner, which is actually much more aggressive (even though in this case, the aggression was verbal).

Although it's understandable that humans sometimes have a reason to become aggressive, our society seems to believe that all forms of canine aggression are wrong, even if the dog is merely defending himself. To understand aggression, you first need to realize that it's very complex: There are many variations, and sometimes what appears to be aggression isn't aggression at all. There are also different ways to help aggressive dogs become more acceptable to society.

Although I've given suggestions for behavior modification below, it is very important to seek professional help should you have issues with aggression, especially aggression against humans. Among other things, a professional can take an objective look at the situation, something that is difficult when we're deeply involved. But as always, be comfortable with the suggestions the professional makes, and don't do anything you deem harmful or dangerous.

Fear-Based Aggression

Fear probably causes at least 90 percent of aggression in dogs. Even dogs who look confident may have begun their behavior because of fear. Sometimes the dog has had a bad experience with a certain group. For instance, if a black dog attacked your dog, your dog may well generalize his fear to include all black dogs. Then, if a black dog approaches, he may snarl or growl. If the dog continues to approach, your dog might well lunge. The poor black dog didn't do a thing to provoke the attack except to draw near, but your dog just doesn't trust black dogs, so he took pre-emptive action to keep him back.

Most dogs who show fear-based aggression have no intention of following through with their display—they're hoping the snarl and show of teeth will work. Actually, most of the time it does. There are some dogs, though, who extend the behavior over time and will actually bite their target.

In Part I, we discussed socialization and how very important it is. Some adolescent and adult dogs miss this socialization period, either with dogs or with people. Single puppies might be very bonded to people, whereas dogs raised in a backyard with no visitors might only be bonded to other dogs. In either case, the adult dog will be suspicious of and uncomfortable around other dogs or people and could very well become aggressive toward them.

Imagine a child had been kept inside a home for 12 years and then was introduced to the big, wide world. Everything would be strange and probably frightening. However, the child might learn to adapt fairly quickly because of language—explanation could lead to understanding. Dogs, though, have to learn through experience alone. Because a dog feels afraid, he may growl or lunge at someone or something that he sees as a threat.

Behavior Modification Method

What, then, should you do with a dog who growls and lunges at strange phenomena, like people in hats, children carrying backpacks, or men with beards? It's tempting—very tempting—to punish the growling. But let's go back to our child.

Perhaps your daughter is afraid of visiting the doctor and screams and fights you every time she goes. For her parent, this is frustrating and embarrassing, and the temptation to punish can be overwhelming. But although physically punishing the child may stop the screaming, it doesn't touch the underlying fear itself. In fact, she could become even more afraid of doctors and may grow to dislike her parent as well! To make the child more tolerant of doctors, we have to think of a way to associate good things with "bad" doctors. This is, of course, why many doctors have candy in their offices.

The dog who is afraid of a particular type of human is growling to try to make the threat go away, and punishing him won't help to treat his fear. Slow exposure, combined with pleasant experiences, is the way to go. You have to change the dog's emotions to help him get through scary experiences. You also have to keep the dog safe from scary strangers, so any behavior modification has to address both issues.

Apply Counterconditioning and Management Techniques

Often, people who have fearful dogs ask guests to give their dog a treat when they come to the door. They're hoping their dog will associate the human with the treat, which is a reasonable assumption. (This is counterconditioning.) But sometimes the dog won't take the treat, or the treat is given after the dog has already growled or otherwise threatened the guest, thus inadvertently communicating to the dog that the growl was appropriate. I generally recommend a combination of management and counterconditioning. Thus, if a dog is frightened of strangers and tends to bark, lunge, or growl when someone comes to the door, a good plan would be to manage his environment—either by putting him in another room for a few minutes, or putting him on a tie-down. When the guests have made themselves comfortable, allow him in to be introduced.

Introduce Strangers Gradually

Dogs, especially frightened dogs, need lots of time to make sure the stranger is safe. The same is true with kids. Adults are big! When they stare down at a kid and hold out their hand, they can be terrifying. A dog's-eye view is pretty much the same as a kid's. Giving both of them time is the first big step toward acceptance. The stranger doesn't have to give the dog food. In fact, I usually discourage that practice unless the stranger is going to be a part of the family, in which case it's just fine.

If strangers dispense food to your dog, a couple of things might happen. First, the dog might take the treat, but because he didn't get enough time to make his own approach, he could actually snap at the stranger. This has happened to me when I'm trying to make "friends" with a fearful dog. I don't do it anymore! Now I let the dog make friends with me. The second thing that could happen is equally unacceptable. The dog could think that people are living candy dispensers and might begin to approach all strangers and mug them for food. Some people do not like dogs and could react fearfully or violently, thus teaching the dog that he was right all along—strangers behave strangely and are scary. If you're still not convinced, think about the human equivalent. We teach our kids never to take candy from strangers. It's just too dangerous. The same goes for our dogs.

Give Him Space

All dogs need personal space, and fearful dogs need more space than most. We humans do too. How close can a stranger or friend get to you before you become uncomfortable? My preferred personal space is pretty large—probably the effect of having 11 brothers and sisters. Other people can easily handle close quarters. Friendly, outgoing dogs tend to need very little space; indeed, they often lie and sleep on top of each other. Shy and fearful dogs, on the other hand, can't handle crowding and may respond aggressively. The solution? Give them space as well as time.

The Bully Syndrome

In contrast to fear-based aggression, the "bully syndrome" is a different story altogether. Bullies usually have the wrong idea about play. They find out that they're stronger than other dogs and they body slam them or roll them over. They usually pick on weaker dogs and leave the more confident ones alone; the weaker ones are much more fun! Think of that kid at school who picks on the smaller, weaker kids. Unfortunately, bully dogs act the same way. It's more show than anything else at first, but the more experienced they become at bullying, the better they get and the more likely it will turn into more violent aggression. This usually happens when the bully picks the wrong dog and that dog retaliates in earnest. There are certain breed types that are more prone to bullying—they often have a high pain threshold and love rough-and-tumble play. Labs, Boxers, Rottweilers, and pit bulls can have a tendency to be bullies unless they're discouraged, as can some terriers.

Some dogs who appear to be bullies are really insecure and scared, so they overcompensate. Sometimes they were body slammed or traumatized when they were puppies. They're often very submissive to more confident dogs but physically dominate weaker, less confident dogs.

Bullies and pseudo-bullies don't necessarily confine themselves to picking on other dogs. They can target family members who appear weak or strangers who give off weak or frightened "vibes." Often the strongest human member of a household doesn't understand why the other members don't just "tell the dog off," not realizing that they can't! It's not in their personalities to do so, and the dog knows it.

Behavior Modification Method

The best method of helping a bully dog learn to be civilized is to take the following combination approach.

❖ Manage his environment so that he can't practice picking on other dogs. Don't take him to dog parks unless you know the other dogs there.

❖ Exercise him on his own or with another dog who can handle his rowdiness. If they get too rough with each other, stop the play (physically, if necessary) and allow a cool-down period before allowing them to play again.

❖ Encourage play with balls or other objects. This is a great way to work off excess energy.

❖ Teach him good manners through extensive obedience work, especially self-control exercises. These include *wait*, *stay*, and *down*.

Leash Aggression

Leash aggression is caused, for the most part, by frustration. It occurs when a dog pulls hard on the leash trying to get to another dog. He's not able to reach the other dog, so he throws a tantrum. The tantrum has all the earmarks of aggression: full tooth display, straining to get to the other dog, dilated pupils, barking, or growling. However, in most cases, if the owner lets go of the leash, the dog will race up to the other dog and introduce himself. Leash-aggressive dogs are often bullies, so their overtures might be quite uncivilized (which certainly could cause a fight).

Leash aggression is very common, and most of the aggression cases I see involve it. Most leash-aggressive dogs are not aggressive off leash but can be holy terrors on leash, scaring the other dog, the other owner, their owner, and themselves. How, then, do you control these dogs? Every time you yank on the leash, you increase his frustration; if you yell, you're barking with him. The best behavior modification technique combines learning to walk on leash nicely and conditioning your dog to realize that other dogs are not as interesting as you are.

Behavior Modification Method

The equipment you use when modifying aggressive behavior should be humane and completely reliable. Make sure that your leash is comfortable to use and doesn't have any cuts in it. Your dog's collar should be secure—it should not come off. I've found that some modern harnesses with a front leash attachment are extraordinarily helpful when modifying leash aggression. When you pull back on a regular collar, the dog tends to pull forward, his head straining toward the oncoming dog. This increases frustration and sometimes aggression. When you use the harness, it minimizes and sometimes even eliminates leash pulling. It also tends to shift your dog's position, pulling him backward in a sort of U-turn. This allows you to get his attention back to you much more easily. Strider was leash aggressive when I got him (as well as anxious!); I attribute much of my success with him to the harness—as well as my fantastic training, of course.

Many people don't know if their dogs are truly aggressive or just leash aggressive. A good trainer can usually find out by testing the dog under controlled circumstances. It's very gratifying to see an owner's relief when he or she realizes his or her dog doesn't want to kill all other dogs. Unfortunately, these dogs are still in for a lot of work to modify the behavior. Just because you know what it is doesn't mean it's easily fixed.

To solve leash aggression, you'll need to teach your dog to walk properly on leash and demonstrate to him that he doesn't have the right to meet every single dog that he sees. Of course, that's easy to say and much harder for a poor owner to do! First, practice lessons including *sit*, *recall* (*come*), and *find it* at home (in a calm location) until your dog is very reliable. It is impossible to teach an exercise when your dog is overly excited, which he will be when he sees another dog.

There are other methods for working on leash aggression, and most require the help of a good trainer. I don't ever recommend physically punishing a dog who has any kind of aggression, including leash aggression. There's a huge chance it will backfire on you.

Going for a Walk

Walk the dog when he is hungry, and take along some delicious treats. He should be on a slack, not tight, 6-foot (2-m) leash. Hold most of the leash in your hand, but make sure that he's not pulling, as tight leashes increase frustration and encourage aggression. When your dog sees another dog, say your dog's name, get attention from your dog, and move as far away from the other dog as you need to (desensitization). Now you have several choices. You can continue to walk by as you give him treats, or you can signal him to sit and reward him. You can also turn away from the other dog and use your *find-it* lesson, which will tend to reinforce a different behavior (that of finding food.) You should be able to keep your dog's attention on you or on the treats on the ground while the other dog passes you or you pass the other dog. If the other dog comes too close, grab your dog's collar and continue to move in an arc away from the dog, keeping your eyes on him and your body between him and the other dog. Stopping sometimes increases the anxiety, while moving more quickly can spark a chase behavior in an oncoming dog.

Repeat this sequence several times, allowing your dog to get closer to the strange dog as he becomes more relaxed. He should get a delicious treat when he sees the other dog and when he gets past the other dog. Remember to try not to sound worried or overly concerned when training your dog to do this. It is just a training exercise, and the more worried you are, the more anxious your dog will be.

Your overall goal is to keep your dog's attention predominantly on you while walking past another dog. He should be rewarded before, during, and after the process. If he begins to show aggression, move rapidly away, but don't yell at him—he may have been pushed past his threshold.

As the behavior becomes more reliable (at least three weeks of consistent rewarding), begin to vary the number and times you reward good behavior. Your dog should view you as a god-like creature who dispenses various types of praise and goodies at different rates.

VERY IMPORTANT NOTE: Desensitization and counterconditioning methods take time to work. We humans tend to get impatient and quit before we see results, or we quit when we get some results but they're not consistent. Repetition is the key to success—think of 1,000 repetitions as your base. In some cases, I've worked with a dog for months or even years, always seeing slow, steady improvement.

Territorial Aggression

We're all territorial—all of us. If you're in your kitchen and you see someone coming up the driveway, you might stop and look out the window—somewhat suspiciously—and wait for that person to either leave or knock on the door. Many people want their dogs to bark when a stranger is at the door or anywhere on the property. Often those same people expect their dogs to recognize that some strangers are okay, like gardeners, contractors, or delivery people. This is asking way too much of your dog! They have no way of ascertaining who's the good guy and who's the bad guy. Some dogs bark at all people or dogs walking by the house, regardless of who they are. Other dogs allow people in the house but won't let them leave. Some bite guests on their way out. Some are quite ferocious behind a fence as they run back and forth.

Behavior Modification Method

To prevent problems such as these from developing, you first need to make sure that the environment is under control. Dogs who set up a lookout perch at the front door or window need to find another place to hang out. Because they won't do it voluntarily, we have to do it for them. Deny access to those areas, block them off, or otherwise make them inaccessible. Find a way to make your dogs happy in another part of the house. What you're trying to do is prevent your dog from practicing sentry duty because as we know, practice makes perfect. If your dog runs the fence line, you'll need to stop this behavior, either by calling him into the house whenever he does it or by not allowing him access to that portion of the yard.

It can be quite difficult to find a way to make your dog happy somewhere else. I found the best way is to teach the dog that his "room" is a place of your choosing, away from the attractions of the world outside. You can do this by having him sleep there, by feeding him there, and by hanging out with him there. If he begins to bark at the door or window, calmly take him from his perch to his designated room. Yelling at him won't work, although that is something we humans must find very reinforcing—otherwise, we wouldn't do it as much!

Another step you can take to control territoriality is to deny your dog "door privileges." Most dogs race to the door when someone arrives, and many bark profusely. It's extraordinarily difficult to try to train your dog while answering your door. In fact, it's usually impossible and leads to yelling, grabbing, and apologizing to guests (who might suddenly decide they'd rather be anywhere else but at your house). A great way around this is to place a little sign at your door telling the visitor you're putting your dog away, or tell them in advance. After your dog has barked at the door, you can cheerfully take him to his "room" and leave him there until you've conducted your business or until things have settled down enough so that he can join you.

Food or Toy Guarding

Some dogs have a hard time parting with what they consider valuable resources, like food or toys. There are several levels of possession problems, from taking the object away to covering it with the body to growling and biting. There are also two different kinds of possession: Some dogs seem to know exactly what they're doing when they guard objects or food, while others appear to go into a state of near hysteria. You can help most dogs learn to share over time. However, if you think that your dog is going to bite someone, seek professional help. Some dogs are just downright dangerous, and you may not have the expertise or time to do the requisite work yourself.

Behavior Modification Method

My favorite way to teach sharing is to help the dog learn that he doesn't have to hold onto the object. In fact, it's in his best interest to let it go. To do that, you need to get his attention. I usually start with a bowl with a few pieces of kibble or a not particularly valuable toy. Just when he's finishing the kibble, approach him with a delicious treat—something out of this world. Put your hand down near his nose and lure him up into a *sit*. When he's sitting, give him the treat. It's very important for him to sit! Do that several times and then slightly increase the value of the food (or toy). I like to go a few feet (m) away from a dog while he's starting to eat and approach as he's finishing because I want him to believe that approaching feet and legs are no threat. When he's sitting up without any cue from you, go to the next step, which is removing the bowl (empty at first) or toy. Go back to your low-value items for this. As you approach, he should sit. Give him the treat at the same time that you pick up the item. Give the item back to him and go away. Repeat. He's now learning several things: First, you are not a threat; second, you have good things to share; and third, he should sit when you approach him while he's got something good.

This method isn't just theory. My rescued Cairn Terrier, Sophie, was extremely possessive and had bitten several people, including me. I tried a variety of behavior modification techniques, and this was the only one that had any lasting effect. Most people can't believe that she was ever possessive.

Owner-Directed Aggression (Dominance)

As we've discussed at length, dogs are part of our families. They need to understand that we make all of the important decisions and that we will take care of them. In some families, the dog ends up feeling that he is running the show and the result can be deadly. These dogs will freeze, growl or snap when the human crosses an invisible line that the dog has set up. For instance, say your small dog is sitting next to you on your couch. You pet him and he snuggles up to you. Then you push him to move him slightly away from you and he growls. He is just telling you that you've crossed the line—if you continue, he might bite. Some dogs will guard their food, toys, or sleeping places, some will guard doorways or other thresholds, and some will not allow their owners to touch or groom them. None of this is acceptable behavior.

In most cases, owner-directed aggression can be successfully modified with management and relationship work. First, the dog shouldn't be allowed to practice the behavior. Thus, if he growls while on a bed or couch, he shouldn't be allowed up. A trailing leash might help with this. If he does get up, you can take the end of the leash and walk away with it. He'll come off the bed or couch with no confrontation, which could provoke aggression. If he guards his food bowl, he should be fed away from the family and the bowl removed after he's finished. And if doesn't allow grooming, that should be stopped until the dog's attitude begins to change.

The second step in this program is the hardest, although at first glance it wouldn't seem to be. Most overly confident dogs love attention on their terms. Although the dog might not allow the owner to approach and pet him, he is likely to seek petting when he wants it. And there's the rub—all attention has to be at the owner's discretion, not the dog's! I generally suggest to my clients that they become very busy—much too busy to give any attention to the dog. When they do have the "time," they should call the dog to them, give him less attention than the dog would like to have, and then ignore the dog again. Many of my clients don't even know how much attention their dog demands. While in my office, I'll start pointing out that their dog is sitting on their feet or leaning on their leg or nudging their hand for caressing. So these people have to first observe the amount of attention they give and then cut way back on it. This takes constant awareness at first but gets easier as time goes on. Just management and withholding attention often solve the problem with adults completely.

It's different, however, with children. They are the most common victims of "disciplinary" bites. A child might approach too quickly or handle a dog too roughly, and the dog will bite the child lightly, generally on the face. Unfortunately, a "light" bite can be serious because human faces are much more vulnerable than a dog's. If a dog has bitten a child, it's very important for the family to see a professional—sometimes, if the situation can't be managed, drastic action has to be taken.

Predatory Aggression

Predatory aggression isn't true aggression, although it certainly looks like it. The behavior is a particularly instinctual one: It's the predator chasing and catching his prey. Unlike most aggression, which is accompanied by a great deal of barking and growling, a predatory dog attacks quietly—there is no noise and no warning. Naturally, one would not warn one's prey before charging. These dogs will vocalize if they're held back by a leash or a fence. In that case, their barks or cries are generally high pitched and very intense. Oftentimes when small dogs are attacked on walks, the attacking dog has mistaken them for prey. Predatory dogs also tend to hang on to their prey, as opposed to diving in and out. Predatory behavior is often sparked by quick movement, such as a cat running or a skateboard or bicycle whipping by.

Behavior Modification Method

There is very little emotion attached to predatory behavior except frustration if the dog can't get to his prey. For this reason, counterconditioning and desensitization are not quite as useful as they are for other forms of aggression, although they do help. As with other problem behaviors, you should associate other, better things with the prey that he wants to get. For instance, if your dog chases bicycles, place yourself a safe distance from a road and ask a friend to ride a bicycle past you. As she passes, give your dog something utterly wonderful to eat and stop as soon as the bike is out of sight. This must be done consistently in a variety of places for your dog to truly understand what you want. And of course, you'll need hundreds of repetitions. If your dog has been a successful hunter of small animals, I highly recommend that you see a very experienced trainer or consultant and that you plan to keep him on leash whenever you're out. This can be a very difficult behavior to modify.

In-Home Fighting

The best advice I can give about multiple-dog problems is to do your utmost to prevent them from occurring. They can be impossible to cure, and like two feuding siblings, sometimes separation for life is the only solution. This is true especially if the two dogs have actually injured each other. Generally, problems arise between two dogs of the same sex. Fighting between members of the opposite sex is unusual, although it occasionally happens. The problem can be very difficult with males, but it's even more intense with females. There's even a saying about it in the behavior world: "Males fight for points, females fight for keeps."

Behavior Modification Method

If your dogs are fighting, first isolate possible causes and triggers. Here are some questions you should try to answer:

❖ Do the dogs get along with each other most of the time?
❖ Do they play or just tolerate each other?
❖ Is there posturing first—do the dogs stare and growl at each other, or do they just start fighting?
❖ Have they injured each other?
❖ Do you or someone in your family have to be present for the fight to occur?
❖ Is one dog much larger than the other?
❖ Is there one clear instigator? (This is difficult to say, usually, because we don't see the first interaction before a fight.)
❖ At what time of day do most fights occur? (Do they occur in the morning, afternoon, or evening?)
❖ Where do they occur? (Do they occur outside of the house, in the house, in doorways or halls, near beds, near food, or near you?)

If only one or two fights have occurred and there were no injuries, you stand a fairly good chance of getting the dogs back together. If they don't become bosom buddies, at least they might become amicable housemates. If there have been multiple fights, it's much more difficult.

Address the Triggers

Your job, once you've answered the questions above, is to address and manage them one by one. For instance, if the dogs fight in hallways in the evening (very common), you might want to have them on tie-downs, chewing on something good. (As parents of toddlers know, late afternoon and evening can be very trying with youngsters—they are rather irritable, to put it mildly.) If you think you have to be present for the fights to start, leave when you feel tensions mount, or implement the following "hot dog" cue. If food is a trigger, by all means feed them separately and remove any signs of food when they've finished. If toys are the trigger, remove all toys except when they're on their tie-downs. If they fight in the bedroom, then remove them both from the bedroom and have them sleep separately (in crates, if necessary). The same is true if they fight when one is in bed and the other approaches, as occasionally happens in my house. Just move their beds when they're not in them.

Ensure Plenty of Exercise

Make sure that the dogs get lots of exercise, together if possible. Take them both to class, or practice their obedience several times a day. You can make them earn their food from you by hand-feeding them bit by bit if you have the time. Play the "fastest *sit*" game (whoever sits first gets the treat first), and do it for everything they consider important: going through doors, getting petted, or getting into a vehicle. By the way, even dogs who fight over food don't do it when it's being hand-fed.

Laughter as a Diffuser

Laughter is one of the best ways to defuse tension in a household. If you, the Ultimate Leader, don't take them seriously, many status-related problems never go anywhere. We even have an exercise called the "hot dog" cue to help keep relationships on an even keel. The cue itself was taught to a good friend of mine by an elderly lady with three pit bulls (all lovingly given to her by her children). It seems the dogs all got along very well most of the time. There was one acknowledged leader among the dogs, and she kept the peace. But as the leader dog got older, things got dicier. The most precious resource was the woman herself, and occasionally when all three were putting their heads on her lap, one of the younger ones would stare at the leader, and all hell would break loose. They'd had a couple of devastating fights, and the woman couldn't stand it anymore. As a result, she developed a signal to help diffuse these situations. As soon as she saw one dog engage another (with "the look") she'd call out in a cheerful voice "Hot dogs!" Then she'd get up and hobble to the kitchen, where she'd open the refrigerator door and pull out three whole hot dogs. After sitting, each of the dogs got one. By that time, they were feeling just fine again—crisis averted!

When I analyzed what had occurred, it seemed to me there were three important components to this exercise. First, the woman had a consistent cue that meant great things to the dogs, and her timing was excellent. It was given at the precursor to the problem, not when the fight had begun, which would have been far too late. Second, she moved. This is important with any in-house dog-to-dog dispute (or child-to-child dispute); you need to move the target resource (her, in this case) and divert their attention from one another. Third, she went to a predictable location, where a certain behavior was required (*sit*) followed by a reliable reward that took a bit of time to ingest. Ever since she so obligingly taught me that exercise, I've used it with many dogs with great success.

Resources

ASSOCIATIONS AND ORGANIZATIONS

Breed Clubs

American Kennel Club (AKC)
5580 Centerview Drive
Raleigh, NC 27606
Telephone: (919) 233-9767
Fax: (919) 233-3627
E-Mail: info@akc.org
www.akc.org

Canadian Kennel Club (CKC)
89 Skyway Avenue, Suite 100
Etobicoke, Ontario M9W 6R4
Telephone: (416) 675-5511
Fax: (416) 675-6506
E-Mail: information@ckc.ca
www.ckc.ca

Federation Cynologique Internationale (FCI)
Secretariat General de la FCI
Place Albert 1er, 13
B – 6530 Thuin
Belqique
www.fci.be

The Kennel Club
1 Clarges Street
London
W1J 8AB
Telephone: 0870 606 6750
Fax: 0207 518 1058
www.the-kennel-club.org.uk

United Kennel Club (UKC)
100 E. Kilgore Road
Kalamazoo, MI 49002-5584
Telephone: (269) 343-9020
Fax: (269) 343-7037
E-Mail: pbickell@ukcdogs.com
www.ukcdogs.com

Pet Sitters

National Association of Professional Pet Sitters
15000 Commerce Parkway, Suite C
Mt. Laurel, New Jersey 08054
Telephone: (856) 439-0324
Fax: (856) 439-0525
E-Mail: napps@ahint.com
www.petsitters.org

Pet Sitters International
201 East King Street
King, NC 27021-9161
Telephone: (336) 983-9222
Fax: (336) 983-5266
E-Mail: info@petsit.com
www.petsit.com

Rescue Organizations and Animal Welfare Groups

American Humane Association (AHA)
63 Inverness Drive East
Englewood, CO 80112
Telephone: (303) 792-9900
Fax: 792-5333
www.americanhumane.org

American Society for the Prevention of Cruelty to Animals (ASPCA)
424 E. 92nd Street
New York, NY 10128-6804
Telephone: (212) 876-7700
www.aspca.org

The Humane Society of the United States (HSUS)
2100 L Street, NW
Washington DC 20037
Telephone: (202) 452-1100
www.hsus.org

Royal Society for the Prevention of Cruelty to Animals (RSPCA)
RSPCA Enquiries Service
Wilberforce Way, Southwater,
Horsham, West Sussex RH13 9RS
United Kingdom
Telephone: 0870 3335 999
Fax: 0870 7530 284
www.rspca.org.uk

Sports

International Agility Link (IAL)
Global Administrator: Steve Drinkwater
E-Mail: yunde@powerup.au
www.agilityclick.com/~ial

The World Canine Freestyle Organization, Inc.
P.O. Box 350122
Brooklyn, NY 11235
Telephone: (718) 332-8336
Fax: (718) 646-2686
E-Mail: WCFODOGS@aol.com
www.worldcaninefreestyle.org

Therapy

Delta Society
875 124th Ave, NE, Suite 101
Bellevue, WA 98005
Telephone: (425) 679-5500
Fax: (425) 679-5539
E-Mail: info@DeltaSociety.org
www.deltasociety.org

Therapy Dogs Inc.
P.O. Box 20227

Cheyenne WY 82003
Telephone: (877) 843-7364
Fax: (307) 638-2079
E-Mail: therapydogsinc@
qwestoffice.net
www.therapydogs.com

Therapy Dogs International (TDI)
88 Bartley Road
Flanders, NJ 07836
Telephone: (973) 252-9800
Fax: (973) 252-7171
E-Mail: tdi@gti.net
www.tdi-dog.org

Training

Association of Pet Dog Trainers (APDT)
150 Executive Center Drive Box 35
Greenville, SC 29615
Telephone: (800) PET-DOGS
Fax: (864) 331-0767
E-Mail: information@apdt.com
www.apdt.com

International Association of Animal Behavior Consultants (IAABC)
565 Callery Road
Cranberry Township, PA 16066
E-Mail: info@iaabc.org
www.iaabc.org

National Association of Dog Obedience Instructors (NADOI)
PMB 369
729 Grapevine Hwy.
Hurst, TX 76054-2085
www.nadoi.org

Veterinary and Health Resources

Academy of Veterinary Homeopathy (AVH)
P.O. Box 9280
Wilmington, DE 19809
Telephone: (866) 652-1590
Fax: (866) 652-1590
www.theavh.org

American Academy of Veterinary Acupuncture (AAVA)
P.O. Box 1058
Glastonbury, CT 06033
Telephone: (860) 632-9911
Fax: (860) 659-8772
www.aava.org

American Animal Hospital Association (AAHA)
12575 W. Bayaud Ave.
Lakewood, CO 80228
Telephone: (303) 986-2800
Fax: (303) 986-1700
E-Mail: info@aahanet.org
www.aahanet.org/index.cfm

American College of Veterinary Internal Medicine (ACVIM)
1997 Wadsworth Blvd., Suite A
Lakewood, CO 80214-5293
Telephone: (800) 245-9081
Fax: (303) 231-0880
Email: ACVIM@ACVIM.org
www.acvim.org

American College of Veterinary Ophthalmologists (ACVO)
P.O. Box 1311
Meridian, ID 83860
Telephone: (208) 466-7624
Fax: (208) 466-7693
E-Mail: office09@acvo.com
www.acvo.com

American Holistic Veterinary Medical Association (AHVMA)
2218 Old Emmorton Road
Bel Air, MD 21015
Telephone: (410) 569-0795
Fax: (410) 569-2346
E-Mail: office@ahvma.org
www.ahvma.org

American Veterinary Medical Association (AVMA)
1931 North Meacham Road, Suite 100
Schaumburg, IL 60173-4360
Telephone: (847) 925-8070
Fax: (847) 925-1329
E-Mail: avmainfo@avma.org
www.avma.org

ASPCA Animal Poison Control Center
Telephone: (888) 426-4435
www.aspca.org

British Veterinary Association (BVA)
7 Mansfield Street
London
W1G 9NQ
Telephone: 0207 636 6541
Fax: 0207 908 6349
E-Mail: bvahq@bva.co.uk
www.bva.co.uk

Canine Eye Registration Foundation (CERF)
VMDB/CERF
1717 Philo Rd
P O Box 3007
Urbana, IL 61803-3007
Telephone: (217) 693-4800
Fax: (217) 693-4801
E-Mail: CERF@vmbd.org
www.vmdb.org

Orthopedic Foundation for
Animals (OFA)
2300 NE Nifong Blvd
Columbus, Missouri 65201-3856
Telephone: (573) 442-0418
Fax: (573) 875-5073
Email: ofa@offa.org
www.offa.org

PUBLICATIONS
Books

Anderson, Teoti. *The Super Simple Guide to Housetraining*. Neptune City: T.F.H. Publications, Inc., 2004.

—. *Your Outta Control Puppy*. Neptune City: T.F.H. Publications, Inc., 2003.

Baer, Nancy, and Steve Duno. *Choosing a Dog: A Guide to Picking the Perfect Breed*. New York: Berkley Books, 1995.

Bailey, Jon S., and Mary R. Burch. *How Dogs Learn*. New York: Howell Book House, 1999.

Budiansky, Steven. *The Truth About Dogs*. New York: Penguin USA, 2001.

Clothier, Suzanne. *Bones Would Rain From the Sky: Deepening Our Relationships With Dogs*. New York: Warner Books, 2002.

Coppinger, Lorna, and Raymond Coppinger. *Dogs: A Startling New Understanding of Canine Origin, Behavior, and Evolution*. New York: Scribner, 2001.

Fisher, John. *Think Dog: An Owner's Guide to Canine Psychology*. North Pomfret: Trafalgar Square Publishing, 1995.

McConnell, Patricia B. *The Other End of the Leash*. New York: Ballantine Books, 2002.

Page, George. *Inside the Animal Mind*. New York: Doubleday, 1999.

Pryor, Karen. *Don't Shoot the Dog: How to Improve Yourself and Others Through Behavioral Training*. New York: Simon and Schuster, 1984.

Pugnetti, Gino. *Simon & Schuster's Guide to Dogs*. New York: Simon and Schuster, 1980.

Rogerson, John. *Training Your Dog. New York*: Howell Book House, 1992.

Sternberg, Sue. *Successful Dog Adoption*. Indianapolis: Howell Book House, 2003.

Wood, Deborah. *Little Dogs: Training Your Pint-Sized Companion*. Neptune City: T.F.H. Publications, Inc., 2004.

Yin, Sophia. *How to Behave so Your Dog Behaves*. Neptune City: T.F.H. Publications, Inc., 2004.

Magazines

AKC Family Dog
American Kennel Club
260 Madison Avenue
New York, NY 10016
Telephone: (800) 490-5675
E-Mail: familydog@akc.org
www.akc.org/pubs/familydog

AKC Gazette
American Kennel Club
260 Madison Avenue
New York, NY 10016
Telephone: (800) 533-7323
E-Mail: gazette@akc.org
www.akc.org/pubs/gazette

Dog & Kennel
Pet Publishing, Inc.
7-L Dundas Circle
Greensboro, NC 27407
Telephone: (336) 292-4272
Fax: (336) 292-4272
E-Mail: info@petpublishing.com
www.dogandkennel.com

Dogs Monthly
Ascot House
High Street, Ascot,
Berkshire SL5 7JG
United Kingdom
Telephone: 0870 730 8433
Fax: 0870 730 8431
E-Mail: admin@rtc-associates.
freeserve.co.uk
www.corsini.co.uk/dogsmonthly

Websites

Nylabone
www.nylabone.com

TFH Publications, Inc.
www.tfh.com

Index

Note: **Boldfaced** numbers indicate illustrations.
Page numbers followed by an "n" indicate that the entry is included in a note.

PHOTO CREDITS

absolute (Shutterstock): 94

aist1974 (Shutterstock): 73

Chris Alcock (Shutterstock): 156

Ugorenkov Aleksandr (Shutterstock): 133

Mikulich Alexander Andreevich
(Shutterstock): 38

Stefan Petru Andonache (Shutterstock): 25

Utekhina Anna (Shutterstock): 61, 178

AnnalA (Shutterstock): 13

Annette (Shutterstock): 27

Anyka (Shutterstock): 31 (far left), 45, 47 (far left), 55 (far left), 65 (far left), 75 (far left), 87 (far left), 105 (far left), 115 (far left), 125 (far left), 137 (far left), 167 (far left), 181 (far left), 189 (far left), 199 (far left), 209 (far left)

Sophie Louise Asselin (Shutterstock): 106 (left)

Denis Babenko (Shutterstock): 136

Stacy Barnett (Shutterstock): 174

Galina Barskaya (Shutterstock): 169 (left)

Casey K. Bishop (Shutterstock): 208

Joy Brown (Shutterstock): 74, 77 (left), 119, 138 (right), 170 (left), 173

Chris Burt (Shutterstock): 169 (right)

cen (Shutterstock): 183 (left)

Andra Cerar (Shutterstock): 190 (left)

Jacek Chabraszewski (Shutterstock): 5 (second from bottom)

Andrew Chin (Shutterstock): 19 (left)

Lars Christensen (Shutterstock): 18

Perry Correll (Shutterstock): 5 (second from top)

Waldemar Dabrowski (Shutterstock): 32 (right)

Dash (Shutterstock): 146

Phil Date (Shutterstock): 141

Julia DeGuia (Shutterstock): 200 (right)

Tereza Dvorak (Shutterstock): 5 (top)

Lisa Eastman (Shutterstock): 23

tim elliott (Shutterstock): 200 (left)

sonya etchison (Shutterstock): 10 (right)

Joy Fera (Shutterstock): 8

Indigo Fish (Shutterstock): 155

Jean M. Fogle@jeanmfogle.com: 198

fotohunter (Shutterstock): 71

Jean Frooms (Shutterstock): 100, 138 (left), 185

Kirk Geisler (Shutterstock): 194

Brad Gibbons (Shutterstock): 56 (left)

Karen Givens (Shutterstock): 148

MANDY GODBEHEAR (Shutterstock): 114

Andreas Gradin (Shutterstock):126

Hannamariah (Shutterstock): 15, 122

Hannimonika (Shutterstock): 2, 16

Perry Harmon (Shutterstock): 31 (second from right), 47 (second from right), 55 (second from right), 65 (second from right), 75 (second from right), 87 (second from right), 105 (second from right), 115 (second from right), 125 (second from right), 137 (second from right), 167 (second from right), 181 (second from right), 189 (second from right), 199 (second from right), 209 (second from right)

Andrew Howard (Shutterstock): 84

Nicole Hrustyk (Shutterstock): 205

Cindy Hughes (Shutterstock): 159

Monkey Business Images (Shutterstock): 210

MY_NEW_IMAGES (Shutterstock): 36

Intraclique LLC (Shutterstock): 162

iofoto (Shutterstock): 9

Eric Isselé (Shutterstock): 31 (far right), 47 (far right), 55 (far right), 65 (far right), 75 (far right), 87 (far right), 105 (far right), 115 (far right), 125 (far right), 137 (far right), 167 (far right), 181 (far right), 189 (far right), 199 (far right), 209 (far right)

Petr Jilek (Shutterstock): 88 (left)

Ian Kahn: 214

Laila Kazakevica (Shutterstock): 134

Alexia Khruscheva (Shutterstock): 63

Iurii Konoval (Shutterstock): 5 (bottom)

Jesse Kunerth (Shutterstock): 91

Erik Lam (Shutterstock): 31 (third from left), 47 (third from left), 54, 55 (third from left), 65 (third from left), 75 (third from left), 87 (third from left), 105 (third from left), 115 (third from left), 125 (third from left), 137 (third from left), 167 (third from left), 181 (third from left), 189 (third from left), 199 (third from left), 209 (third from left)

Philip Lange (Shutterstock): 116 (right)

Sergey Lavrentev (Shutterstock): 59

fotograaf limburg (Shutterstock): 123

Maxim Urievich Lysenko (Shutterstock): 31 (second from left), 47 (second from left), 55 (second from left), 65 (second from left), 75 (second from left), 87 (second from left), 105 (second from left), 115 (second from left), 125 (second from left), 137 (second from left), 167 (second from left), 181 (second from left), 189 (second from left), 199 (second from left), 209 (second from left)

NatUlrich (Shutterstock): 78 (right)

ncn18 (Shutterstock):104

Dwight Lyman (Shutterstock): 77 (right), 130

Natalia Sinjushina & Evgeniy Meyke (Shutterstock): 20 (left)

Andrzej Mielcarek (Shutterstock): 66 (left)

Kati Molin (Shutterstock): 203

Pedro Jorge Henriques Monteiro (Shutterstock): 166

Lee O'Dell (Shutterstock): 88 (right)

Justin Paget (Shutterstock): 78 (left)

Steven Pepple (Shutterstock): 206

Margot Petrowski (Shutterstock): 110

Michael Pettigrew (Shutterstock): 95, 112

Rick's Photography (Shutterstock): 212

David L. Lewis/Wishing Well Productions

(Shutterstock): 153

Scorpp (Shutterstock): 60

Nata Sdobnikova (Shutterstock): 56 (right)

kristian sekulic (Shutterstock): 216

Shutterstock: 5 (third from top), 51, 62, 106 (right), 143, 161, 190 (right), 192

Joanna Stachowiak (Shutterstock): 187

Claudia Steininger (Shutterstock): 170 (right)

Colton Stiffler (Shutterstock): 180

Alexey Stiop (Shutterstock): 97

Jeffery Stone (Shutterstock): 6

SueC (Shutterstock): 66 (right), 81

Svemir (Shutterstock): 48 (left)

RedTC (Shutterstock): (right)

Laurent Renault (Shutterstock): 76

Tina Rencelj (Shutterstock): 197

Albert H. Teich (Shutterstock): 69

Nikolai Tsvetkov (Shutterstock): 48 (right)

April Turner (Shutterstock): 28

Alice Mary Herden Vision-Vault LLC (Shutterstock): 32 (left)

Vukoslavovic (Shutterstock): 131

Charles White (Shutterstock): 20 (right)

Whitechild (Shutterstock): 103

Ivonne Wierink (Shutterstock): 10 (left), 116 (left), 135, 150

sandra zuerlein (Shutterstock): 121, 126 (right)

front cover: Hannamariah (Shutterstock) (top, far left); soya etchison (Shutterstock) (top, second from left); Shutterstock (top, second from right); Gorilla (Shutterstock) (far right); Andresr (Shutterstock) (bottom, far left); neelsky (Shutterstock) (bottom, middle); Anna Jurkovska (Shutterstock) (bottom, far right)

back cover: Eric Isselé (Shutterstock)

All other photos courtesy of Isabelle Francais and TFH archives

DEDICATION

This book is dedicated to parents of both species and their kids, including my own daughter, Robin, who taught me a great deal.

ACKNOWLEDGMENTS

It is impossible to properly thank all of the people and animals who have helped me learn, either personally or through their books. The staff and volunteers at the Marin Humane Society, of course.

I'd also like to thank my friends and fellow trainers inside and outside the shelter, including Sue Sternberg, Patricia McConnell, Kathleen Chin, the late John Fisher, John Rogerson, Pia Silvani, Pam Reid, Suzanne Hetts, Mary Lee Nitschke, Ian Dunbar, Suzanne Clothier, and Terry Ryan, just to name a few. I am grateful to the Association of Pet Dog Trainers (APDT), a wonderful organization (formed by Ian Dunbar) that advocates cooperation in the dog training profession, as well as providing continuing education. Not only is it a great resource, it also provides a forum for those of us who just can't stop talking "dog."

I would also like to thank my editor, Stephanie Fornino, who helped me take this manuscript and actually make a book out of it while remaining cheerful and pleasant through it all.

And of course, I have to thank the dogs—all of them—for being who they are. Just Perfect.

ABOUT THE AUTHOR

Trish King, CPDT, CDBC, is the Director of the Animal Behavior & Training Department at the Marin Humane Society (MHS) in Marin County, California. King teaches workshops and seminars on behavior, canine management, temperament assessment, and handling difficult dogs. She established the Canine Behavior Academy at MHS for new or interested trainers, which covers training theory and techniques, handling dogs, and teaching people. She is also an instructor for the Officers Training Academy at MHS.

King is a member of the panel that put together the Delta Society's *Professional Standards for Dog Trainers: Effective, Humane Principles* and has spoken nationally at several well-known venues, including conferences held by the Association of Pet Dog Trainers (APDT), the Humane Society of the United States (HSUS), and the American Humane Association (AHA). King is also a member of the International Association of Animal Behavior Consultants, Inc (IAABC).

NATURAL with added VITAMINS
Nutri Dent® MD
Promotes Optimal Dental Health!

Dogs Love'em!™
AVAILABLE IN MULTIPLE SIZES AND FLAVORS.

Nylabone®
Trusted For Over 40 Years

MADE IN THE USA

Our Mission with Nutri Dent® is to promote optimal dental health for dogs through a trusted, natural, delicious chew that provides effective cleaning action...GUARANTEED to make your dog go wild with anticipation and happiness!!!

Nylabone Products • P.O. Box 427, Neptune, NJ 07754-0427 • 1-800-631-2188 • Fax: 732-988-5466
www.nylabone.com • info@nylabone.com • For more information contact your sales representative or contact us at sales@tfh.com   TS446